"Reinhold Niebuhr was the strongest critic of racism—within the historical and cultural limitations of what he understood it to be—of any major theologian of his time, and Ronald Stone is more deeply learned about Niebuhr's life and thought than any theological scholar of our time. This book is a welcome treasure trove of all that Niebuhr said about racism, drawing winsomely upon Stone's storehouse of memories of the later Niebuhr."
 —Gary Dorrien, author of *A Darkly Radiant Vision:
 The Black Social Gospel in the Shadow of MLK*

"Ronald Stone's new book on Niebuhr's approach to racism brings the important and disturbing message that current conflicts over racism within American religious and political life follow a century-long paradigm that is hard to shake and that leads one to ask whether Euro-Americans have the substance to face and conquer their apparent genetic racism in the post-George Floyd period of our history."
 —Matthew Lon Weaver, author of *Religious Internationalism:
 The Ethics of War and Peace in the Thought of Paul Tillich*

"Ronald Stone provides helpful analysis here of twentieth-century ethicist Reinhold Niebuhr's responsiveness to American racial problems. By filling in gaps in Niebuhr's record on racial concerns and by drawing attention to sometimes underemphasized aspects of his racial commentary and activism, this book broadens the basis for assessing Niebuhr's contributions to one hundred years of American racial thought and practice."
 —R. Drew Smith, professor of urban ministry,
 Pittsburgh Theological Seminary

REINHOLD NIEBUHR AGAINST RACISM

REINHOLD NIEBUHR
against Racism

RONALD H. STONE

with research assistance from
MARK RUSSELL

CASCADE *Books* • Eugene, Oregon

REINHOLD NIEBUHR AGAINST RACISM

Copyright © 2024 Ronald H. Stone. All rights reserved. Except for brief quotations in critical publications or reviews, no part of this book may be reproduced in any manner without prior written permission from the publisher. Write: Permissions, Wipf and Stock Publishers, 199 W. 8th Ave., Suite 3, Eugene, OR 97401.

Cascade Books
An Imprint of Wipf and Stock Publishers
199 W. 8th Ave., Suite 3
Eugene, OR 97401

www.wipfandstock.com

PAPERBACK ISBN: 979-8-3852-1034-3
HARDCOVER ISBN: 979-8-3852-1035-0
EBOOK ISBN: 979-8-3852-1036-7

Cataloguing-in-Publication data:

Names: Stone, Ronald H., author. | Russell, Mark, research assistant.

Title: Reinhold Niebuhr against Racism / Ronald H. Stone ; with research assistance from Mark Russell.

Description: Eugene, OR : Cascade Books, 2024 | Includes bibliographical references and index.

Identifiers: ISBN 979-8-3852-1034-3 (paperback) | ISBN 979-8-3852-1035-0 (hardcover) | ISBN 979-8-3852-1036-7 (ebook)

Subjects: LCSH: Niebuhr, Reinhold, 1892–1971—Political and social views | History—United States—20th Century | Christianity and politics

Classification: BR115.P7 S755 2024 (print) | BR115.P7 S755 (ebook)

Contents

Acknowledgments | ix
1. Introduction | 1
2. Race at Bethel | 14
3. Detroit Mayor's Committee on Race | 17
4. Bethel Church Dispute | 41
5. *Moral Man and Immoral Society* | 43
6. Building Institutions in the South | 47
7. Palestine-Israel | 59
8. Martin Luther King Jr. | 63
9. Realism and Idealism | 65
10. Jews and Christians | 71
11. Civil Rights Act of 1957 | 77
12. The New Frontier | 80
13. Birmingham Bombing | 85
14. *Mississippi Black Paper* | 89
15. The Seminar | 92
16. After King's Murder | 97
Bibliography | 109
Index | 115

Acknowledgments

PERSONAL APPRECIATION OF REINHOLD Niebuhr's permission to quote from any of his writings or personal conversations as I worked on my first book/dissertation on him in 1968–71. Recognition that he wrote on his professor and to his mind never misrepresented his thought even when he disagreed. Thanks to the Citizens Research Council of Michigan for permission to reprint the "Mayor's Committee on Race Relations," 1926. Thanks to the successors of the Advisory Council on Social Action of the United Church of Christ for the 1968 essay, "The Negro Minority and Its Fate in a Self-Righteous Nation," which I edited and published. Mark Russell, Pittsburgh Theological Seminary librarian, was of immense assistance in finding and reproducing Niebuhr's essays on race.

1. Introduction

THE OVERCOMING OF THE evil heritage of slavery and racism in the United States remains a major issue. The task of ending racial separation and racism in the Christian churches is still before us. The major Christian commentator on public policy and church issues of the last century is Reinhold Niebuhr. Recently his contribution to ending segregation and improving public policy for the black population has been questioned by both black and white critics. This book's thesis is that a fuller reading and understanding of Niebuhr on race reveals a rather complete theory of combating white racism for our own time.

A former pastor, Dr. Robert Chesnut, raised the question of Niebuhr on race after reading James A. Smith's critique of Niebuhr in *The Christian Century*. Smith had suggested that the lack of discussion of race relations in *The Irony of American History* indicated Niebuhr's insensitivity to the race issue at the time. I was not aware of Smith's contributions to improving race relations. But of course more relevant was that in that period Niebuhr wrote about fifteen essays or editorials on the race problems of the country. Even more to the point was that the book was not a history but a comment on irony and particularly relevant to the rivalry with the Soviet Union. Even more important was that American race history for Niebuhr was a tragedy and not particularly ironic. After I commented on Smith's work, Chesnut asked me to write a response to it. I followed through in a discussion of Smith in *The Christian Century*.[1] My

1. Stone, "Niebuhr's Record on Race."

colleague on Pittsburgh Presbytery's Peacemaking Committee, the Reverend Matthew Fricker, raised the same question with me after reading James Cone, *The Cross and the Lynching Tree*,[2] and one white graduate and her black partner who had founded the Neighborhood Academy to prepare black students for college asked me about Cones's criticism of Niebuhr on race. Their school became one of the more successful projects to fight the consequences of racism in Pittsburgh.

I taught in James Cone's seminar at Union Theological Seminary the last few years before Professor Cone's death. We would always have lunch and discuss Niebuhr early in the afternoon, and after the late afternoon seminar we would finish the day with wine and more dialogue in his apartment. Once we discussed writing jointly on Niebuhr and race, but we decided our perspectives based in our respective experiences differed too much. He needed to have his say. This is mine. Cone came to Union Theological Seminary in 1969 as assistant professor and I left for Pittsburgh from Columbia University to become associate professor. Since that time we occasionally discussed Niebuhr, our respective books, and the church. He used my books in his class, and I assigned his books at Pittsburgh Theological Seminary. Professor Walter Wiest and I agreed to use his first book *Black Theology and Black Power* while we were picketing downtown businesses to help construction guilds accept blacks as apprentices in 1969. This book continues the dialogue from our friendship. Niebuhr grew from the influences of his southern Illinois town to a sophisticated public intellectual based at Union Theological Seminary and Columbia University. He developed from a social gospel liberal, to a Marxist Christian critic, to a dialectical crisis Christian theologian, and to the retired, disabled, pragmatic liberal I met in the 1960s.

Here his thoughts on race are presented chronologically, which is the best way, if not the only way, to understand Niebuhr. The purpose of the book is dual. I want to respond to the critique of Niebuhr on race relations, and I also to present his writings on race to show a rather complete theory of how Christians and

---

2. Cone, *Cross and the Lynching Tree*.

1. Introduction

well-intended humanists can use his writings as guides to improving the American racial situation. A thesis of my response is that the critics have not read several of Niebuhr's writings on race relations, and very few of them have discussed his major projects on racial reconciliation. In particular, they have not read his work on the Mayor's Inter-racial Committee in Detroit in 1926 nor have they read his review of the Kerner Commission report on the racial riots of 1968. This book uses these two reports as bookends on his remarkably thorough work on race relations. James Cone read the later commission report but undervalued Niebuhr's foreword to the *Mississippi Black Paper* of 1968, as well as most of his writing on lynching. Despite Cone's thorough work he also relied on my earlier comments on "The Negro in Detroit" report. The two pieces by Herbert Edwards missed most of Niebuhr's significant work on race. Niebuhr's white critics seem to deplore Niebuhr's lack of interest or development of the subject, but they fail to provide evidence of having studied Niebuhr's major works on race. So this book addresses race relations from a Christian perspective in terms of Niebuhr's actual writings and works, for presentation of a major contribution to the subject to help us overcome the white sin of supremacy and discrimination against our siblings. I must leave it up to the reader of this volume to decide whether the impressive biography of Niebuhr was accurate enough when it recorded: "civil rights had never been one of his preoccupations, though he always scorned racial prejudice."[3] A major conference on Niebuhr's thought and relevance published in 1989, which opened with a paper by Professor Richard Fox, had almost no reference to his career-long fight against racism in America.

The mayor of Detroit asked this well-known minister and frequent writer for the Detroit newspapers to chair the race relations commission necessitated by the race riots over integrated housing and trials of 1925. Niebuhr's sermons denouncing the Ku Klux Klan had been featured on the front pages of two Detroit newspapers regarding the election, making him a known quantity in Detroit on the race issue. The report compiled a set of

3. Fox, *Reinhold Niebuhr*, 282; Neuhaus, *Reinhold Niebuhr Today*.

recommendations for changing Detroit's response to the racial crisis. Though Niebuhr's specific recommendations and tone might have changed over the years as his vocabulary certainly altered, the commitment to a comprehensive response to the evil of racial structures and prejudice remained constant. Fred Butzel, a Jewish lawyer, became a close friend of Niebuhr in social causes, and Niebuhr credited Butzel for helping him immensely on the Mayor's Inter-racial Committee. So this volume, also, remarks on Niebuhr's struggle to protect Jews from racism.

The second document studied is his letter to the Council of Bethel Church criticizing their action of refusing membership to black people (1928). Though church integration was a rare occurrence in the United States, membership denial on the basis of race violated the very meaning of church.

Niebuhr was discouraged after his experiences in Detroit and on leaving for New York he published "Confessions of a Tired Radical." He criticized liberals for their lack of action and their liberal confessions. He pleaded for the understanding that group prejudice was nearly universal and that practical steps had to be taken to alleviate the sins against black people. In his tiredness he hoped for renewed energy to pick up the struggle.

By 1930 he was back in the struggle speaking on unionization in the South and leading workshops in the South for both blacks and whites. His narrative of this visit emphasizes the charming character of the South for whites in both the introduction to the essay and in its conclusion, while mentioning lynching briefly. Characteristically he dealt with racism in both the South and North as his next essay illustrated. He refused to give Yankees any room for a false sense of pride in race relations.

His "Brief Comments" on lynching is interesting for its early date, and it is followed up later as a priority for legislative action when that seemed possible. Similarly his piece on Mississippi is interesting as it precedes his stronger piece by over thirty years.

The wartime essays on race move to the more inclusive problems of wartime Japanese and Jews. His lectures at Union Theological Seminary on race often referred to both Jewish issues and

1. Introduction

black discrimination in their American histories. The outcome of the war in Europe was decided by late 1942, and his essays of 1944–45 returned to the relevance of the church in the race relations issues. The greater tension in the relations between the races was discussed in "The Negro Issue in America" and "Christian Faith and the Race Problem" in 1945. He was deeply disappointed by the lack of response by the church, but he remained hopeful. He could not understand during the war that the hope would be partially fulfilled by the black church in the next decade.

His militancy against racism increased in the 1960s during the period in which he found the Kennedys and President Johnson encouraging race relations in the United States to be radically changed. *The Mississippi Black Paper*, and *The Fate of the Negro Minority* in this decade, though seldom read by his critics, marked this militancy.

My son, Randall Stone, thought I should introduce this book with a narrative on my remembrances of participating in the struggle for the freeing and empowering of blacks. James Cone's autobiographical, posthumous volume, *Said I Wasn't Gonna Tell Nobody*, reinforced that advice. My great-grandfather, born shortly after the Civil War, indicated our family were Republicans because we had been followers of Abraham Lincoln. His mother came from a distinguished family of Quakers who had followed our great-grandfather as county commissioner. They had fled Wisconsin after being harassed as abolitionists. The came to Humboldt County, Iowa, in a covered wagon and homesteaded across the river from great-grandpa Stone who, as the head of the county commissioners, gave abolitionist speeches and bid the men of the county go off to war. He received letters notifying him that two of his cousins, one at Gettysburg and one in Virginia, were killed in the war. The Stone and Knowles wedding followed Lucy's teaching in country schools of which great-grandfather Stone was superintendent. Most of this history was shared with me with the expectation that I would follow the path. Some of this history was given to me by my grandfather as we sat on the front steps of our house in the village of Dakota City, named for the earlier neighbors to the land. One of my earliest memories is of his story of giving chickens to starving Dakota Sioux in the cold winters of the 1870s; meanwhile an airplane flew over our heads as we listened to tales of the frontier.

There were no black people in Humboldt County, Iowa, unless one counted seasonal workers who came to the county fair to manage or ride the race horses or to erect the Ferris wheel and merry-go-round. The town had a John Brown Park and a statue of a Union soldier on a column in the Union Cemetery. We all learned to sing "John Brown's Body Lies a-Mouldering in the Grave" in public school and "Onward, Christian Soldiers" in church. The town's history was awash in the distant stories of its utopian founders who, after failing in their Unitarian attempts to build the Harvard of the Midwest, moved on to other adventures in California. I cannot affirm my ancestors were integrationists because there were no blacks in Humboldt County. Dad made a few negative remarks about black people. But when we visited his brother in Indianapolis, he would go visit Cotton with whom he had worked on auto shows. On returning to our hotel from a game at Soldier Field, he did not hesitate with his strong hands to crush a fire that had started on a little black boy's clothes from a sparkler.

I began to meet black youth as a boxer in the Des Moines Golden Gloves when I was a senior in high school. My dad's brother tried to dissuade me from participating as he feared the urban youth would not fight fairly. Years later I found similar fears in British boxers on the Oxford team who sought my counsel as to how to fight black boys. In fact there is no counsel to be given.

Morningside University in Sioux City, Iowa, had a few blacks from Sioux City and others recruited for athletic teams, and I became friends with black boxers at the police gym where we trained. The one student from Panama joined in our Methodist Student Movement local integrationist acts in barber shops and skating rinks. The restaurants were already integrated. Through actions by my friends I became vice chair of the Iowa Methodist Student Movement and chair of their race relations project in 1958. The concluding rally brought Methodist black activists up from

1. Introduction

colleges in the South and it threatened the university president. As the managing editor of the college paper, I reluctantly had to challenge him by reporting on his moderate refusal to deny us the use of the campus, and our rally and workshops went on. Several Methodist groups from across the state reported on their movements to integrate businesses serving the campuses. I followed up with a race relations sermon in my home church in Humboldt, Iowa. My paraphrase of Jesus's word in 1 John 4:19, "That if you claimed to love God, but did not love your neighbor, you lied," then became, "If you did not support the present civil rights struggle, you lied in your affirmation of loving God." It did not go over well in that middle-class Republican church. A cousin wrote me that the crowd at the county fair claiming I was a communist disturbed him. My father, who had come to church that day, was very perturbed by my sermon and warned me about preaching on race relations, and he expressed his anger to my brothers.

I was proud to be accepted by Union Theological Seminary, but the financial officer wrote me that she doubted we could afford it. Probably as a newly married couple my wife and I could not have, but we moderated our joint educational goals until my scholarships a few years later made it possible for my wife to complete her Morningside University degree with hours transferred from City College of New York and Barnard. I saved the financial officer's letter for years thinking I would read parts of it when I was inaugurated as president of Union. When chosen as a distinguished alum, I shared the wording with Serene Jones, then serving so well as president. Before we left for New York, my summer job was running a camp for poor whites, Native Americans from the reservation, and black kids from the city. Having completed my term as a student pastor to a church near the Missouri River, the Methodist Church also assigned me to clean up a troubled congregation a little further south on the river before heading off to New York City. My work there involved persuading farm workers to join the congregation. The district superintendent, a Union graduate, had given me his copies of Niebuhr's *The Nature and Destiny of Man*. I read both volumes that summer in the mornings, saving my visitations to the farmers until the afternoons.

Part of the trouble at the second congregation arose from a dispute over how close to build the new outdoor toilet to the church. Should it be built close because of the Iowa winters? Or should it be built further away because of Iowa summers? Of such matters is a student minister's time taken. In my previous church we had built its first indoor toilets. After calming the church, partially with flannel board stories for the kids, we packed our meager possessions in a 1954 DeSoto and headed for New York City. Driving though the Holland Tunnel I hesitated on the Manhattan side until a large policeman approached and bellowed: "Where are you going Iowa?" Following his directions we arrived at Claremont and 122nd Street where a kind professor directed us to the dolly to unload our meager possessions. Relevant to the theme of this book, I arrived as a committed follower of Martin Luther King Jr. and as a believer that through the church we could change race relations in the United States. As a leader in that Methodist Student Movement I had read the books by the authors who influenced James Cone in his early years: Mays, Kelsey, Thurmond, King, and others. I had some experience in the nonviolent use of force for social change in favor of American blacks. That experience would get deepened at Union.

I interviewed for a student educational experience at a Methodist church in Harlem that had pictures of its famous son, Sugar Ray, on the hall walls. But I ended up at Riverside Church working under the direction of a black youth minister, Bob Polk. There I helped the integrated youth plan worship. I also coached boxing and a basketball team. We nearly got into a gang fight in the Baptist church beside the Brooklyn Bridge. One of my boxers made the finals of the Golden Gloves at Madison Square Garden. But he lost by making every mistake I tried to coach out of him. Years later I met him on the subway and the shape of his cauliflower ears made me regret that he had gone professional. One time I led a kid outside who was disrupting a worship service. He said, "But teach, I haven't seen a girl in six weeks." My further queries produced

1. Introduction

the information that he had come to youth worship that evening after having been released from Rikers Island. The youth work at Riverside Church was followed by a summer job at a children's center in Harlem. It was a wonderful summer taking the kids to zoos, museums, swimming pools, Bear Mountain State Park, and other attractions including the United Nations. My favorite kid challenged me for not forewarning them of the UN trip because he would have dressed up. He was correct. Years later when I took seminary classes to the United Nations I always warned them to dress formally.

The Union Seminary ethos led me into demonstrations. A memorable event was picketing Woolworth's five-and-dime on 125th Street in Harlem to support the students picketing in the South. Frequent trips to Washington, DC, involved lobbying senators and more demonstrations, usually sleeping on the pews of New York Ave. Presbyterian Church. So public demonstrations were part of my education. Eventually this led to my organizing with Union students, CORE, and Hospital Workers Local an occupation of the South African Embassy over Mandela's sentencing. Wes spent the night in the New York City jail (the Tombs). The next morning we were taken to a hearing. The judge suggested a date for the trial, admitting that Adlai Stevenson's order to remove us would require the South African Embassy to appear in court. I suggested his recommended date would be hard for me. He asked why, and I told him I would be late for my first teaching position. He inquired where and what I would be teaching. I said my first college teaching would be at Morningside University in Sioux City, and that I would be teaching Western civilization, ethics, and international relations. He responded, "This court would not want to deprive Iowa of your wisdom on these subjects." He postponed the trial and I was only one day late for my first teaching position. I followed this up by publishing an issue on South African apartheid in *Social Action*, dialoguing with David Rockefeller and bank officials on divestment, writing for a presidential candidate on the subject, and later teaching an ethics class on apartheid in Pittsburgh for two years with a South African.

Out of many demonstrations, one memory stands out. I helped organize a student and Harlem Methodist demonstration in Pittsburgh outside the Penguins' Civic Arena where the Methodist General Conference was holding its meeting. The relevant issue was the structure of the church regarding its Central Conference, which was its wholly black conference. We were lobbying to integrate it into the full church. Walking in the picket line, I was approached by the new district superintendent of the Western Iowa District: "What are you doing here, Stone?" I explained we were hoping to move the Methodist Church into the future as an integrated church. I asked him to join the picket line, and he refused. I never heard from the Methodist Church in Iowa officially after that encounter.

Courses at Union Seminary and Columbia University led me to specialize in the study of ethics and international relations, and as an assistant to the secretary of the United Church of Christ in international relations to work with the United Nations and the church. Professor Roger Shinn asked me while I was studying at Oxford to return to New York to assist him and Reinhold Niebuhr. Few other offers could have lured me away from philosophy at Oxford, the proffered captaincy of the boxing team, and the beloved town where my son was born. I never would have chosen Reinhold Niebuhr as my mentor if I had been called to work in race relations. But I was not, and my interests in political philosophy and international relations were also his specialties. Lobbying for voting rights legislation while Johnson was president led to demonstrating in front of the Lincoln Memorial for four hour shifts for a few days until the voting legislation was passed.

It is important to understand specialization in academia. Reinhold Niebuhr did political ethics and international relations, especially war and peace; James Cone did systematic theology with an emphasis upon black power. I need to mention that Professor Cone shared with me that he did not know if the dissolution of the Central Conference of the Methodist Church had a positive outcome. The overcoming of the racial separation in the Methodist Church had been a major issue for me as chair of the social action

1. Introduction

committee of Union Theological Seminary in the mid-1960s. James and I became acquaintances when he moved to Union in 1969, and I was leaving Columbia University for Pittsburgh. A few years later he warned me that Professor Marcus Barth told him that my contract with Pittsburgh would not be renewed as I was too much of an activist for the good of the school. The warning gave me a chance to organize, and soon I was appointed full professor at age thirty-two. Later Cone asked me to join him in teaching Niebuhr's thought in his seminar on Niebuhr and I visited Union years before his death to participate in the seminar for an afternoon. I smiled upon hearing a black professor say how disappointed he was that Cone refused him admission to sit in the class. I regarded his syllabus on Niebuhr as the most complete I had ever seen even though I taught a course on him every other year for thirty-four years. Cone used my books in his class, and I used his first book in 1969 and others later. I taught seminars on Niebuhr every other year, on King regularly, twice on Niebuhr and King, and once on King and Gandhi.

Earlier at Pittsburgh Seminary, we had struggled to integrate the faculty. We had done pretty well in admitting the small black student population of the metropolitan area. The black dean and I had agreed to try to increase the mission of the seminary to serve more black students and to orient the seminary more toward the city. One of my black students from the urban ethics class had advanced to chair of the Allegheny County Council and eventually he appointed me to the ethics commission of the county. Unfortunately the dean moved, leaving only one black professor, Samuel Roberts. We taught together until he was recalled to Union Theological Seminary. Pressure from Presbyterian black clergy and the generosity of the Pittsburgh Foundation led to my negotiation among the active parties until the president of the seminary took over and I shifted to the search committee. The president preferred Ronald Peters from the University of Massachusetts and we eventually brought him to the seminary. He assumed the course I had taught in urban church and society and also developed a very strong metro-urban center, which strengthened the black studies at the seminary and the seminary's relevance to the city significantly. Years later the president and I got into conflict over the role of black faculty at the seminary. Our faculty fight led other faculty to emphasize the issue. So by the time I retired in 2005 we had four black faculty and a black dean of students. The seminary could not retain all of them, but it has maintained at least two black faculty since and recently added a black president to lead the institution.

After Niebuhr's death in 1971, several scholars chose to criticize Niebuhr's writings on race as too moderate, uninspired, uninformed, too few, or simply lacking. These writers, as far as I can discern, did not know Niebuhr personally. Some of them have not read deeply in Niebuhr, and most of them seem ignorant of major activities of Niebuhr in race relations. Of course a gigantic figure like Reinhold Niebuhr inspires many different interpretations. Some of the criticisms are fair. A few that are fair may not be important given Niebuhr's theology and ethics. But I suspect Niebuhr gives us a relatively complete suggestion for strategy of overcoming racism as far as we can now overcome it. If a major American theologian had it just about correct on race, that is an important story to tell. Rather than denigrate our fathers in social ethics it maybe more helpful to learn from them and figure out how applicable they may be now decades later. Perhaps I should conclude this personal story by saying that I am still demonstrating and organizing for justice in voting for blacks on the steps of my church in my eighty-third year and supporting the anti-racism movements of 2022–23 in the street.

Cone's writing on Niebuhr in *The Cross and the Lynching Tree* is among the most profound on the subject. If read following his first chapter on lynching, it is persuasive. Cone still regarded Niebuhr as the best of the white theologians on the subject. I absorbed his critique of Niebuhr as also a critique of myself, Cone's friend and colleague. He noted my early reading of the chapter and I wish I had read his chapter on lynching at the same time. He criticizes both John C. Bennett and me for our defense of Niebuhr on the subject of race. Cone's theology is unique and I appreciate much of it. As an integrationist I appreciate Martin Luther King

1. Introduction

Jr. more, and Niebuhr's dialogue partner, James Baldwin, less than Cone. If at points I supplement Cone's research it is for the sake of an alliance between whites and blacks, which I value.

2. Race at Bethel

UPON COMPLETION OF TWO degrees at Yale, Reinhold Niebuhr was asked by the German Evangelical Synod to accept the pastor's position at a small mission church in Detroit in 1915. He argued for a better salary, because his mother, Lydia, depended upon him for support. The church membership consisted of sixteen families. He was pleasantly surprised at his first service to find a large crowd of mostly aged or very young worshipers. When he asked about the strange makeup of the congregation he was told the retirement home and the orphanage had been invited for the occasion. The congregation grew and by the time of his departure for New York in 1928 it had grown to over six hundred members in a handsome new building.

    His small German-speaking denomination urged him to work as executive secretary for its War Welfare Commission. This responsibility took him to training camps, to consultations with the denomination's chaplains, and to represent his denomination at ecumenical war council meetings. All of this work was hardly represented in his published diary reflections on his ministry. He reserved the responsibilities for Bethel Church on the weekends. Some members of the Evangelical Synod allowed their German origins to influence their opinion of the war. Niebuhr became their critic, arguing for the loyalty of the church members to the nation and Wilson's causes. He also asked to resign the position of war secretary and to join the struggle as an army chaplain. The denominational leaders refused his proposal to resign, and he continued in the role until the end of the war. His family and

2. Race at Bethel

eventually an assistant pastor covered the weekly responsibilities at Bethel Evangelical while he served first as war secretary and then as a speaker at regional and national church events. Soon he was popular, speaking in college chapels, and advising in various church advisory roles. His role as a writer grew particularly in the *Christian Century*. In that role he became known as a critic of the Ford Motor Co. and as a writer on social issues.

Reinhold Niebuhr's writing does not include reflections on race relations until his closing years at Bethel Evangelical Church. Then the listing of convictions about race relations developed. As a German-speaking youth from Lincoln, Illinois, through a German college and seminary, probably more should not have been expected until his move to Detroit, Michigan, where the black population doubled during his ministry (1915–28). The poverty of the South and the wages of the booming auto industry lured the Great Migration. Though he wrote a lot of essays during those years, race relations was not a topic in his publications except for an essay on German Americans. He had developed his English at the Yale Divinity School, and he wrote out of his immense energy and financial needs to support his family. However, it was a particular political battle that drew him into race relations. He attended a few conferences on race relations in the 1920s and one that his church committee sponsored had over five hundred participants, but basically the race question did not appear in his writings until the KKK became an active political force in 1925 in Detroit. Most politicians stayed away from addressing the powerful Klan. It could elect senators and congressmen and fill the streets of Washington, DC with three hundred thousand white-clad and hooded men. A famous trial was held in Detroit in which Henry Sweet was found not guilty after shooting a white protester from a mob that was attacking his brother's newly purchased house in a white neighborhood. Clarence Darrow, fresh from the Scopes trial, had defended Sweet, attracting the attention of the national Klan. Funds were poured into the city to encourage the Klan-supported Protestant against the Catholic incumbent mayor in 1925. The election was close and the Klan dreamed of a victory in Detroit, the fourth largest city in the United States. Ministers from progressive backgrounds joined together in their sermons to condemn the KKK. Their sermons were commented on in the front pages of *The Detroit Free Press* and *Detroit Times*. References to Niebuhr condemning the Klan bigotry as a Protestant heresy were reported first in the articles. John W. Smith, the mayoral incumbent, appreciated Niebuhr's support in the narrowly won election. Within a few months he appointed Niebuhr to chair the interracial committee. Niebuhr's energy gave fire to the committee, which had languished under a couple of previous leaders. The acquisition of a grant to undertake sociological research on the race problem in Detroit encouraged Niebuhr, who desired to combine scientific research with the moral recommendations of his committee.

3. Detroit Mayor's Committee on Race

THE SOCIOLOGICAL REPORT "THE Negro in Detroit"[1] covered 469 pages in twelve sections. While it recognized the quality and meagerness of housing for black people as a central issue, it neglected to mention the mob, the fatal defense of Dr. Sweet's home, or the famous trial. The report did include one other racial protest involving a shooting and reported on several cases in which racial agitation followed a black person who was buying a home in a white district. It discussed the nature of the report, population migration, and industry, thrift, and business of black people, before discussing housing, and then proceeded to health, recreation, education, crime, religion, community organization, and welfare of black people. Niebuhr's Mayoral Interracial Committee[2] started with housing, and then pursued the same topics as the sociological study through sixteen pages. Neither report expected to side with black people or racists. They rather accepted the realities of prejudice and discrimination in Detroit and tried to reach proposals in Niebuhr's report to ameliorate the situation. The study was the work of the Detroit Bureau of Governmental Research and much of it consisted of reports of different governmental bureaus. Interviews of black people in both the criminal interviews and the housing interviews revealed the squalor of black living conditions in the city. Issues we would expect to be covered by reports

1. Niebuhr, "Negro in Detroit."
2. "Report of the Mayor's Committee on Race Relations."

today, like violent racism on the part of police or white ownership of the slum housing, which lacked sewage or running water, were not thoroughly discussed, although mild reports of prejudiced police violence and murders were not totally neglected. The pages on housing referred to the large number of homes rented to black people by Jews and noted that earlier the area had been largely inhabited by Jews. The terms "Negro" and "colored" were used interchangeably in the report while distinctions between the "new" Southern Negroes and the "old" Northern Negroes were maintained pretty consistently throughout the sociological report. The report summarized the squalor in which the immigrant blacks lived and the oppression of the police. The 1920s were regularly reported as a time of affluence for the American people without much reference to the poverty of black people or their lack of buying power of the products they produced. Particularly the interviews the researchers obtained with blacks in Detroit during this time of watered-down stock prices, middle-class affluence, riotous parties, and new mansions draw tears from sympathetic readers even now almost one hundred years later. One-third to half of their salaries from Ford would cover the rent for a family in black areas. Women were usually unemployable in the factories and their earnings as laundresses or prostitutes left little for their children. Those newly arrived from the South were often uneducated beyond the third grade and ill equipped for Northern urban living. The older Detroit blacks distinguished themselves from the newer migrants from the South. Neither in the social research nor the mayor's report was the subject of integration of churches mentioned. It appears that the subject was not seen as relevant to Detroit in 1926–27.

Niebuhr had, in England in 1926, argued that the Ford Motor Company should be socialized. Here he had to deal with the employment officer of the Ford Motor Company on his committee dominated by Detroit lawyers. Many of those on welfare had worked only a few months for Ford before being unemployed. He learned existentially the thesis of Ernst Troeltsch that in society compromises with the Christian ethic is the most that can be achieved. He evolved a friendship with a righteous Jewish lawyer, Fred Butzel, which endured and he attributed much of the committee's work to him. Still a black bishop was vice-chair and the lawyers and executives of Detroit had their own impact on the committee. Niebuhr was chair, but in committee work no single influence can be attributed. The committee report was not radical, but then few other Christian ministers have chaired urban city government committees. I was more critical of the committee's work before I chaired Allegheny County's ethics committee. The report called for the establishment of a permanent racial relations committee in government. Changes in practice in city departments were recommended to better the black citizens of the city. Black groups were urged to improve the appearance of their neighborhoods without reference to the owners or the lack of income for black people. The report noted white fear, not financial reality, was blamed for drops in real estate values, noting black people often paid more for poor accommodations than other citizens. Real estate and banking practices called for reform, but not for legislation. Police reform and the removal from African neighborhoods of prejudiced police were recommended. The low percentage of black people on the police force called for correction. Also in education black people were not permitted into positions in leadership and their numbers in the teaching ranks were inadequate. Similarly, few black teachers, nurses, or other professionals were employed in Detroit. Of course, the problems were exacerbated by blacks from the South having received less education with lower standards. In industry, discrimination in both unions and employers were recognized. Abuses by undereducated black religious leaders were noticed and financial and sexual mismanagement characterized the existence of many black churches. Reforms except for interdenominational organization and white church support for black churches were meager. The survey of the education of black ministers found few had obtained college, university, or seminary education. Half the black population belonged to churches, but as of yet there was not adequate space for them. There was no mention of the desirability of integration of the churches or of their usefulness in achieving justice. The drift toward cynicism on the part of Niebuhr was encouraged by the failure of the churches in race, employment, and war.

> Report of the Mayor's
> Committee on Race Relations
> DETROIT, MICHIGAN[3]
>
> Embodying findings and recommendations based upon a survey of race conditions in the city, undertaken in 1926
>
> Mayor's Race Committee:
>
> Rev. Reinhold Niebuhr, Chairman.
>   Pastor, Bethel Evangelical Church
> Bishop William T. Vernon. Vice-Chairman
>   African Methodist Episcopal Church
> Dr. E. A. Carter, Secretary
>   Physician
> Fred M. Butzel
>   Lawyer, Butzel, Levin and Winston
> Fred G. Dewey
>   Lawyer, Campbell, Dewey, Stanton and Bushnell
> Frederick C. Gilbert
>   President Vulcan Mfg. Co.
> Donald J. Marshall
>   Employment Officer, Ford Motor Co.
> W. Hayes McKinney
>   Lawyer
> Mrs. Charles Novak
> Mrs. C. S. Smith
> Walter H. Stowers
>   Lawyer
> Jefferson B. Webb
>
> **Introductory**
>
> The following findings and recommendations of the Mayor's committee on race relations are based on a survey made for the

---

3. See "Report of the Mayor's Committee on Race Relations."

3. Detroit Mayor's Committee on Race

committee by the Detroit Bureau of Governmental Research. The immediate occasion for the work of the committee was a series of race difficulties in the summer and fall of 1925. Since the World War the colored population of the city has grown from 10,000 to 80,000. The rapid expansion of the colored community has created so many social problems involving all sections of the community that it was felt that these problems could be faced intelligently only if the detailed facts could be ascertained. The survey was made in the summer months of 1926. Both funds and time were limited so that the survey is not by any means exhaustive. It did, however, give the committee and will give the public a fair and more adequate picture of race conditions in the city than has been available hitherto. Since the completion of the survey the committee has met weekly and these findings and recommendations are the fruit of its deliberations. While the committee has arrived at many specific recommendations involving official policy and governmental action it has always been conscious of the fact that the final solution of all the problems which have been revealed must wait upon the cultivation of better understanding and the diminution of prejudice in the public at large. The committee hopes that its efforts may finally issue in the organization of a permanent race commission which will enlist the cooperation of colored and white leaders in the city. Such a commission would have the double task of initiating educational projects through clubs, schools and churches by which better feeling between the races will be created; and of exercising vigilance over the policies of public and semi-public agencies in order that the conscience of the community may be focused upon and work for the elimination of the causes of race friction and race discrimination as they are revealed from time to time in the life of the city.

Housing

1. The demand for an Interracial Committee grew out of an unfortunate series of clashes between the races in this city, which was due to the inevitable and necessary expansion of the Negro community. The situation is, therefore, sufficiently charged with emotion to make it improbable that any recommendations of this Committee will meet the unqualified

favor of extremists on either side. The constitutional rights of the Negro have been bought at too high a price to make any suggestion which might seem to imperil these rights acceptable either to the colored or to fair-minded white people. On the other hand, the mere insistence on legal rights will not avail to solve the acute housing problem which faces the community in general and the Negro community in particular. The task of the Committee, as it conceives it, is therefore, to suggest solutions which, while not imperiling legal rights, will also not ignore the cultivated or instinctive race prejudices of large sections of the community or the fear that race migrations may result in loss of real estate values, as real factors in the situation.

2. Our survey shows conclusively that in many instances where the colored population filtered into white residential sections making them ultimately colored sections, there was no loss of real estate value and in many cases the rentals and sale prices increased. We believe that frequently where property depreciation does occur it is due to the expectation that it will occur, that is, the hysteria in the neighborhood in which the penetration has begun causes many homes to be thrown upon the market and depreciation becomes inevitable. In many instances where infiltration is slow, colored persons are accepted by the white neighbors in a friendly, even though somewhat formal manner. When a colored family moves into a white neighborhood the outcome seems to depend upon the character and attitude of the nearest neighbors. If such white neighbors are tolerant and civil, the resulting situation is not bad; if, however, without any attempt to appraise the colored people as individuals, an antagonistic attitude is assumed by the whites, or if the particular colored family offends against the established standards of the neighborhood, friction is inevitable.

3. A general campaign of education is necessary to urge on colored people the special desirability of keeping their houses painted and their yards in attractive condition so that colored sections should compare favorably with sections occupied by white persons of corresponding economic status. A similar emphasis upon the personal appearance and demeanor of colored people and their children is equally desirable.

3. Detroit Mayor's Committee on Race

4. Peoples of various races have a natural tendency to live in their own communities and this tendency is on the whole conducive to community peace. If Negroes seem inclined to move into white districts it is frequently due to their desire to gain equal civic facilities with whites. When streets in Negro districts are kept in repair as they are in white districts and when equal sanitary, educational and other facilities are made available for them, there will be a more general tendency on their part to remain where they are or when they move to expand by group rather than by individual action. If this general tendency is to be encouraged it is particularly important that Negro centers be freed from vice and crime conditions by proper police action.

5. In order to make the acquisition and maintenance of good standards of Negro housing possible, it is necessary for banking and loaning institutions to be more liberal in their attitude towards Negro loans. In justice to the banks it must be said that property occupied by Negroes has frequently been dilapidated or in sections already deteriorated before the Negro influx. Furthermore, there is a natural fear that the Negro influx might depreciate property values in white sections. When it is once clearly shown that Negroes are moving in groups and taking especially good care of their homes and that the City Government is keeping up standards of sanitation, policing and schooling in Negro districts, it is quite probable that the banks will cooperate more willingly in assisting Negroes to own their own homes and acquire real estate.

6. The responsibility for encouraging Negro groups in the proper care of their property and for exercising vigilance upon governmental agencies that flagrant neglect of Negro districts may be prevented should rest upon a permanent committee of white and colored persons, about which we expect to make further recommendations.

7. At the present time it is especially desirable that the authorities without delay take cognizance of the unsanitary conditions prevailing in some Negro subdivisions, particularly in the Eight Mile district where there is neither adequate water supply nor sewage disposal. Many of the dwellings in the St.

Antoine district are unsanitary beyond redemption. The Board of Health, which is at present making a special survey in this district, should have the hearty support of the administration and the public should it decide to condemn and raze some of the buildings in this district. The committee here in before indicated should assist in finding homes for families rendered homeless by such condemnation and razing.

8. Because of the urgency for the need of better housing among Negroes, we suggest that the city administration survey the possibility of a housing scheme designed to offer credit facilities to home builders of such small income that their building enterprises offer no attraction to commercial bankers and builders.

9. Large industrial concerns would find it profitable to interest themselves in the housing of their employees and encouragement should be given to Negroes working in large factories to obtain housing near their work. Some of them at present, spend as much as four hours a day traveling to and from their work and waste energy that could be better devoted to improve efficiency in the factory and in the home.

Crime and Police

1. It is obvious from our report that general prejudices from which minority races throughout the world suffer at the hands of the majorities are operative in this city, coloring the minds both of the public and of the officials who are charged with the administration of justice, so that exact and even justice for the members of the minority race (in this case the Negroes) is still an unattained ideal.

2. The percentage of Negro crime is unquestionably higher than the average crime rate of the city. Undoubtedly this is partially due to the incomplete adjustment of the recent southern immigrant to the industrial urban life of the north. The great proportion of single men and women among the recent migrants and the consequent instability of home life, over-crowding and lack of facilities for wholesome social life, poverty and illiteracy, all these social and economic

3. Detroit Mayor's Committee on Race

factors contribute to a high crime rate which the superficial observer will attribute solely to racial factors. The problem of reducing crime in the colored community is therefore only partly one which pertains to the courts and the police. The decrease in lawlessness in the Negro community must finally wait upon a completer adjustment of the newer migrant to the social conditions of the city, to the establishment of stable home life, to the integration of the Negro into the industrial life of the city, to the raising of educational standards and the elimination of abject poverty. A large number of Negro crimes are undoubtedly crimes of passion rather than crimes of premeditation. The lack of emotional stability to which this points will undoubtedly be gradually eliminated as the cultural and educational standards of the race rise.

3. There is evidence that in many cases Negroes are treated with undue severity, not to say brutality, by the police. The assumption among many police officers, that Negro criminals offer a special peril to the life of the officer and that consideration of self-defense, therefore, justify unusually precipitate action in firing upon Negro criminals, is not borne out by the facts. This unjustified assumption has resulted in needless loss of life on occasion of Negro arrests. This condition will probably not be remedied without much greater vigilance on the part of the department in disciplining officers guilty of unwarranted brutality. There is some evidence that the prosecutor's office is unduly lenient in exonerating police officers who have killed persons in the process of arrest. While we recognize the difficulties confronting the prosecutor's office in investigating the killing of criminals and alleged criminals investigating such killings and initiating prosecution where the facts warrant.

4. Contrary to a general impression in the colored community the number of officers of Southern birth and heritage has not been unusually high in the Negro districts, nor can such officers, according to our evidence, be held responsible in an undue proportion of the cases in which officers shot colored people. Nevertheless we recommend that the police department formulate a policy of excluding from precincts in which colored people predominate, officers whose social background or

previous history prompt them to an undue measure of race prejudice. We further believe that it might be wise policy for the department to investigate the personal bias of officers it intends to use in colored districts.

5. The number of colored policemen in the Detroit Department is unusually low. Until recently there were only 14. The cities of Boston, St. Louis, Chicago, Pittsburgh and Los Angeles have from two to nine times as many Negro officers in proportion to the force as Detroit. It would be a distinct advantage to increase this number materially. The experience of other cities, so far as we are able to ascertain, does not justify the belief that Negro officers are unduly lenient with Negro criminals. On the other hand the employment of Negro officers in Negro districts excludes the factor of race prejudice both in the minds of the public and among the police of cases of conflict between police and Negro persons. Furthermore, the employment of a larger number of Negro officers would improve the morale of our rapidly growing Negro population.

6. Our study shows considerable variation in the outcome of Negro cases before the courts in both felony and misdemeanor cases and the proportion of Negro convictions in some courts is seemingly high. This fact would seem to warrant the conclusion that there is a lack of adequate consideration both on the part of juries and judges. Some unfairness is undoubtedly the result of a lack of adequate legal counsel owing to the poverty of the ordinary Negro defendant. The facts cannot be established with sufficient clarity to warrant a recommendation.

7. We call the attention of the Community Union to the fact that inadequate institutional facilities for delinquent girls creates a special problem in the case of colored delinquent girls.

Business and Thrift

1. In view of the size of the city and the numerical strength of the colored population, home ownership and business enterprise among colored people is disproportionately low. The rapid expansion of the colored community through recent migration undoubtedly accounts for this fact. It would be an

3. Detroit Mayor's Committee on Race

advantage both to the city and to the colored community if home ownership with its responsibilities were encouraged.

2. The banks have no special facilities for dealing with colored credit applicants and determining upon their responsibility and honesty. This, together with the fear of shifting real estate values have made the banks slow to grant loans in the colored districts. If home ownership is to be encouraged it is necessary that the banks pursue a more generous policy. Some branch managers in colored districts are rendering a splendid service by seeking out the more responsible and capable customers and helping them to lay the foundation for bank credit. It is to be hoped that such a policy will be more generally adopted and encouraged by the banks of the city. It will contribute much to the stabilization of the colored population and the development of leadership. Moreover, the more general employment of trained colored help would probably develop and encourage Negro business for the banks.

3. There seems to be an almost universal complaint on the part of the banks that Negro accounts are overactive. There are many instances of savings accounts opened on one pay-day and closed before the next pay-day, thus greatly increasing bookkeeping expense. This practice greatly prejudices the standing of Negroes in the eyes of bankers. Colored organizations might well devote some attention to the task of teaching their members correct methods of banking. If depositors are taught to maintain their accounts indefinitely and discouraged from withdrawing the entire account when money is needed, the relation between banks and colored customers will be greatly improved.

4. It is gratifying to note that there are a number of instances of very successful business enterprises being conducted on special lines by colored people. It would be well if these successful ventures could be brought to the more general attention of the public through the press and otherwise. It has been disappointingly difficult to ascertain the facts in regard to the amount, extent and variety of life insurance carried by colored people. It is desirable that a further survey be made of this field

and that the indifference of life insurance companies toward colored business be overcome.

Education

1. While the percentage of retardation among colored children is unusually high there is evidence that much of it is due to the lack of educational facilities in the southern districts from which most of the Negro migrants have come. There is considerable difference in the percentage of retardation between children of northern and of southern birth, so that an improvement in the standing of colored children may be expected as the benefits of superior educational advantages make themselves felt in the first and the second generations.

2. The Board of Education is expanding its classes for children who are retarded three years or more. A further development of such classes will greatly benefit Negro children who have come to the city without educational advantages. It is taken for granted of course that such classes, while of special advantage to Negro children of southern birth, will always be available for retarded children of any race.

3. The number of colored teachers employed in the schools of Detroit is not great. While the committee would not suggest that racial groups are entitled to teachers in proportion to the number of children of the group in the schools, it is nevertheless obvious that a larger number of colored teachers could profitably be employed in the school system. There is no evidence of overt discrimination against colored applicants for positions. The small number of teachers is undoubtedly due to the fact that the majority of our Negro population have had so few educational advantages that the group as a whole is handicapped in producing its quota of teachers who are able to pass the high requirements of the Detroit schools.

The committee does not presume to say that lack of discrimination on the part of the School Board and the administration inevitably implies that there are no cases of covert discrimination in the application of general policies to specific cases by individual administrators. Race prejudice

3. Detroit Mayor's Committee on Race

being what it is, such discrimination probably does occur in individual instances. There are no colored teachers in high schools and none in supervisory positions. The committee hopes that the school administration will make every effort to give capable and experienced teachers of the colored race a fair opportunity to aspire to such positions. No doubt both the schools and the individuals for such preferment would have to be carefully chosen at first.

4. The pressure of time has made our survey on education rather incomplete compared with other aspects of race relations.

Health

1. Colored patients are admitted to most of the hospitals of the city. Where discrimination occurs it is usually sporadic and is frequently due to specific cases of irritation on the part of white patients. There is a tendency in some hospitals to keep the number of Negro patients down to a certain proportion of the total bed capacity. In the case of a few private hospitals colored patients are either not admitted or their reception is very generally discouraged.

2. Facilities for the care of unmarried Negro mothers are inadequate. This is particularly true of cases involving venereal diseases. It is to be hoped that the proposed united campaign for women's institutions will supply this lack in the institutional equipment of the city.

3. The Board of Health is to be commended for its program of maternity education and its encouragement of the hospitalization of maternity cases. This has probably been the chief cause of an appreciable decrease in infant mortality in the Negro community from 1920 to 1925.

4. In view of the fact that the total hospital bed capacity is inadequate for the needs of the city, it would be an advantage to the city as well as to the colored community if Dunbar Hospital could be materially enlarged, or possibly a new hospital project, catering particularly, but not exclusively, to colored people,

could be initiated. It might be possible to interest philanthropic friends of the colored people in such a project, provided the highest scientific standards for the institution could be guaranteed. This end might be achieved by the organization of a mixed directorate and mixed staff at least for some years to come. Among other advantages such a project would help to solve the problem of providing adequate training for a larger number of colored interns and colored nurses. The hospital could function without eliminating the need of or discouraging the service of other hospitals to the Negro people.

We suggest that the Board of Education might profitably detail some competent person to make a careful investigation of race conditions in our schools, as they involve both teachers and pupils, to the end that where suspicion of discrimination has been created it may be allayed where it is unjustified and its cause may be abolished where it is justified.

Recreation

1. The Department of Recreation has an excellent record of service to the colored people. It has made its facilities available to them and has increased its Negro force to keep pace with the growing colored population. On the whole, there is comparatively little race friction in the recreational life of the city under the department's supervision. The chief exception is in the matter of swimming in indoor pools where mixed bathing unfortunately becomes the occasion of unpleasant incidents. Difficulties seem to be confined to certain indoor pools and have not occurred at outdoor beaches. The department is making every effort to preserve the legal rights of the colored group and at the same time to make its facilities available for all groups with the least possible friction.

2. There is a serious lack of summer camping facilities for Negroes, particularly for women and children. We suggest that the Recreation Department and existing private and public agencies, both colored and mixed, give this matter their immediate attention. Race prejudice in country communities adjacent to possible camp sites adds special difficulty to the problem of providing fresh air facilities for the Negro people of the congested districts.

3. Detroit Mayor's Committee on Race

3. We suggest that institutions such as the Y. M. C. A., which possess camping facilities, make these available for certain periods for colored people under the same conditions which apply to their other camp periods. The acquisition of additional camping facilities for the use of colored people by such agencies, is also highly to be desired.

4. Since the High street community center is to be razed we recommend that the Department of Recreation and the administration take steps to provide an adequate substitute for this social center in a district heavily populated by Negro people. If the Ginsburgh library is to be abandoned by the Library Commission we suggest that this building, with the addition of a gymnasium and swimming pool, might well serve this purpose.

Industry

1. The progress of the Negro in the industrial life of the city, following the large migrations since the war, has been most creditable. Many of the largest employers of labor report that their efficiency equals that of other workers in the same type of work. They are gradually making their way into the skilled trades. Employers who follow the practice of not employing Negroes might well consult the experience of those employers who have employed Negroes in large numbers and usually report very favorably on their general efficiency. There is little evidence of wage discrimination against Negroes in the factories, partly, no doubt, because most Negroes are employed in the unskilled trades in which wage rates are low for both white and colored.

2. Negro women are under special disadvantage in securing employment in this city. There is comparatively little employment for women of any race in the metal industries of the city and in the commercial establishments the general race prejudices of the public have resulted in almost universal discrimination against colored saleswomen. Domestic service, which in other cities offers some outlet for colored women workers, is also restricted here. The moral consequences of this situation are very grave.

3. Commercial employers of broad social sympathies could render a great service to the welfare of the race and the entire community if they would undertake to open up such opportunities for employment for colored women as would be least likely to aggravate the prejudices of the public.

4. We suggest that social agencies adapted for the task, preferably the Y. W. C. A., be entrusted with the organization of a vocational school for colored girls, specializing in domestic science, the household arts and home nursing. There is at present a lack of training among colored girls and there is no agency to develop and to certify the ability of applicants for positions.

5. Trade school facilities, especially adapted to the needs of colored boys, is urgently needed in the city and we suggest that the Board of Education give this matter its attention.

6. While there is some objection in labor circles to the subsidizing of the employment office of the Urban League by the employers, there is, on the other hand, a widespread discrimination, either overt or covert, against Negroes in many labor unions, which forces the Negroes to secure employment wherever or however they can. Unions which do not discriminate against Negroes report that they are loyal and cooperative members of the union.

The Church

1. Since the church is the most important institution in the life of the Negro people it is very necessary that the various church groups cooperate more effectively in their common tasks. While cooperative ventures have developed materially in recent years, denominational feeling still seems to run very high in the Negro churches. As a result the Negro churches are not as effective in meeting their common problems and those of the Negro community as they would be under a policy of more generous cooperation. We suggest that steps be taken by the leaders of the Negro churches to organize an effective agency of church cooperation.

2. Such an agency of the Negro churches might do much to eliminate irresponsible religious organizations which enjoy a mushroom growth in the city. These organizations generally lack stability and discipline in their group life; the moral fruits of their religious fervor are frequently jeopardized by a type of hysteria which issues in social phenomena of dubious ethical value. The leadership in these groups is usually without adequate educational equipment and free of any kind of supervision or discipline. These irresponsible churches tend to work an injustice upon the well disciplined and ably led Negro churches by seeming to justify judgments on the part of casual observers against the Negro church as a whole, which the total facts do not warrant.

3. The Negro churches are in desperate need of more equipment. Only a few of the churches have facilities for their social life. Many of the congregations are able to accommodate only a fraction of the people who desire to worship with them. Their need ought to be a serious challenge to the white churches which annually raise thousands of dollars not only for foreign missions but for church extension in our own city and for other home missionary tasks. Most of the larger denominations do support one or two Negro churches in the city. The Episcopal Church recently contributed $60,000 to the erection of a church house for its Negro parish. The Congregationalists are helping their Negro church acquire a suitable edifice. The Presbyterians and Methodists also support one or two Negro congregations. The Detroit Baptist Union is, however, the only denominational body which gives financial aid to Negro churches belonging to its general denominational group but not in organic connection with the denomination. Since the largest Negro churches are members of autonomous Negro denominations it is quite clear that the aid of white churches to single Negro churches, organically related to them, will not solve the church issues.

Welfare and Community Organizations

1. A survey of the welfare organizations reveals inadequate facilities for the care of the children of colored working mothers. We suggest that the Urban League and the

Community Union give particular attention to the establishment of additional day nurseries, accessible to colored children.

2. Several private agencies having a large percentage of colored clients need additional colored workers. We suggest that the Visiting Housekeepers' Association, the Visiting Nurses' Association, the Children's Aid Society and the Girls' Protective League secure additional competent colored social workers.

3. In view of the favorable experience of private social agencies and the Department of Public Welfare in the use of colored social workers, we suggest to the Juvenile Court that it reconsider its present policy of not using colored social workers. They might be particularly useful in dealing with colored clients in the Mothers' Pension Department and in treating delinquency.

4. Some of the outlying Negro districts, particularly River Rouge-Ecorse, Inkster, Thaddeus-West Jefferson, Wabash, Eight Mile Road, Nevada-Conant and Quinn Road, are not receiving the attention from welfare organizations which older and more centrally located districts enjoy. We suggest that the Community Union survey these districts as quickly as possible in order to determine their social needs. We also believe it necessary that the Urban League take steps to organize community organizations in these districts, through which both the general needs of the community and specific cases of distress may be brought to the attention of the proper authorities and agencies.

5. The records of the Department of Public Welfare indicate that a very large number of Negroes, most of them recent immigrants from southern rural homes, are not yet adjusted to northern urban life and are frequently reduced to dependency. While immediate aid is given to them and is no doubt necessary, it may easily aggravate pauperization, particularly the erection problem of the Negro churches. We believe that this is a problem which ought to seriously engage the white churches of the city and we recommend that a special meeting

3. Detroit Mayor's Committee on Race

of the white and Negro church leaders be held to survey the whole problem.

Since many in this class take dependency for granted. More trained Negro case workers, experienced in the problems of this group, are necessary so that the case load of each worker may be reduced sufficiently to permit attention to the problem of individual and family rehabilitation. We suggest that the Department of Public Welfare consider the advisability of organizing and consulting with case committees of representative Negro citizens.

6. The Young Women's Christian Association is so constituted that practically all Negro women of Detroit are eligible to its membership. Religiously it is sympathetic to the ideals of an overwhelming majority of Negro women. Both its recreational and educational program need expansion which is possible, however, only through the provisions of more adequate physical facilities. The present equipment is hopelessly inadequate for its task and the staff is too small. It is to be hoped that the building campaign of the Y. W. C. A. will make adequate provision for the expansion of the facilities of the Negro branch.

7. The Urban League is the one recognized organization for official co-operation of white and colored groups in the city. It also offers a common meeting ground for all colored groups and it is the organization through which special projects for improving health and recreation and for fostering art and other forms of expression have been initiated.

The work of the Urban League is carried on in a small downtown office on St. Antoine street where the executive and employment office is located and in the Columbia community center where there are facilities for recreational, clinical, musical and other group activities and where, upon occasion, professional, business and college alumni groups meet. The Columbia community center is the only social service center entirely manned by Negroes which is not connected with specific religious organizations. In view of the large growth of the city and the proportionately larger growth and complexity of the Negro group the physical equipment of the Urban League is totally inadequate. A well planned and furnished building for the League is an urgent necessity. Considering the newness of the Colored community and the relative poverty of its members it is earnestly to be hoped that some generous friend of the Negro people will undertake the financing of such a building.

Niebuhr's speaking on race expanded to include secular organizations as well as familiar church commitments. He brought the new work home to Bethel in four sermons in January of 1927: January 2: "Race Relations in Detroit"; January 9: "Where Shall the Negro Live?"; January 23: "What about Negro Crime?"; January 30: "The Race Problem of the Church." He announced them as being based on the sociology research prepared for the Mayor's Interracial Committee. The theme was carried in his lecture at Elmhurst College: "The Challenge of Race to the Christian Conscience." Before he left Detroit he sponsored a Sunday evening lecture and discussion of lynching. According to the FBI files, the *Daily Worker* recognized Niebuhr as a leader in the drive for antilynching legislation. He was still working on it in 1951 when he urged senators to give priority to the antilynching legislation, which he believed could win support from even Southern forces. Anti-lynching legislation had to await the presidency of Joe Biden to succeed in the federal courts. This early work needs recognition in all discussions of Niebuhr and race. Though his early work was before the birth of his most famous critics on lynching, the 1950 discussion is also in the relevant period in which it should be noticed.

His book from the period, *Does Civilization Need Religion?*,[4] did not refer to the Mayor's Committee or his work in race relations. The next book, *Leaves from the Notebook of a Tamed Cynic*,[5] only had one day's notice on the racial crisis. There are a few other sentences, but no major discussion of the subject in his early books. It was clear that racial discrimination was a terrible

---

4. Niebuhr, *Does Civilization Need Religion?*
5. Niebuhr, *Leaves.*

3. Detroit Mayor's Committee on Race

sin and in clear opposition to the Christian gospel. His article in the *Christian Century* after the committee had completed its work, "The Confessions of a Tired Radical,"[6] distanced himself from liberals who, in his opinion, delighted in confessing the sin of racism as displayed by the middle class, but wasted their time in meetings without organizing practical measures.

He was of the opinion that most groups preserved their own homogeneity by criticizing the deficiencies of other groups. He often experienced Nordic Protestants separating themselves from their own groups by condemning their group's sin. He suggested Nordic Protestants may have inordinate group pride, but he offered examples of other groups' racial pride. Groups in control seemed to exhibit the worst racial pride, but few groups were innocent of the sin. "The sins that the white man has committed against the colored man cry to heaven."[7] Reflecting on his mayor's report he was willing to suggest that even established Northern black people have trouble accepting the recently arrived blacks from the South. He tended to see racial pride as a universal or almost universal phenomenon and the solutions to it resided in practical action rather than racial specific critique. Even Gandhi's critique of Western man against the more spiritual Eastern man was criticized in "Confessions of a Tired Radical" despite his great respect for Gandhi. The religious racism of India awaited the 1948 division of Muslims and Hindus for confirmation. Niebuhr did not open up the subject of caste founded in discrimination on the basis of color. The human nastiness about race resided within the human heart and love of one's own group's virtue.[8] He hoped soon to move beyond his tiredness. He also regarded racial prejudice as stemming from the broader human tendency to overidentify with one's own group and to despise other groups. It is obvious from his publications that major themes of his writing were labor problems and the dangers of international relations. The struggle among

---

6. Niebuhr, "Confessions," 1046–47.
7. Niebuhr, "Confessions," 1047.
8. Niebuhr, "Confessions," 1046–47.

classes was as important or more so than race relations for him. He described himself as a realistic follower of the social gospel.

None of his writing at this time expected much action on the race issue from the churches. Particularly Protestantism suffered from its individualism and sentimentality. The Mayor's Committee did not regard the churches in Detroit as a major force for change. The churches Niebuhr experienced were more priestly than prophetic. The occasional prophetic preachers had to learn to be tactful and understand that churches were controlled by the white middle classes. Even his relationships with black militants like Albert Cleage—whose church, Shrine of the Black Madonna, was founded in the 1960s long after Niebuhr had left Detroit—failed to provide strategy for change. The church three blocks up the street from Niebuhr's Bethel Evangelical Church failed to provide hope for the black church's intervention and the shrine lasted only a few years. Cleage said he had met often with Niebuhr and that he was most in debt to Niebuhr for his realistic perspective. Cleage thought Martin Luther King Jr. needed more of Niebuhr's realism, and he claimed Niebuhr had led him out of his social gospel heritage to a more realistic understanding of Christianity. Niebuhr stayed closer to King's philosophy than Cleage did, as he affirmed black nationalism. Cleage expressed his enthusiasm for Niebuhr's focus on power which was required for any desirable social change.[9] Cleage tended to give Detroit credit for teaching Niebuhr realism; Niebuhr credited World War I for his change toward realism. Writing shortly after his report on race in Detroit he described the addition of realism to his social gospel inheritance.[10] He also credited Bishop McConnel, a social gospel advocate, with showing him how to add statesmanship to his struggle for social justice. His major concern about the social gospel was that it inherited too much of American optimism, even approaching sentimentality. He never abandoned his social gospel inheritance. He added to it political realism, and some of that realism came from the recognition of the total failure of the white Christian churches to address

9. Ward, *Prophet*.
10. Niebuhr, *Leaves*.

3. DETROIT MAYOR'S COMMITTEE ON RACE

racism before the 1950s. Even in his final biographic reflections he noticed his social gospel orientation.[11] Neither American economics nor politics were influenced very much by the Christian gospel. Niebuhr had been interested in politics earlier as he chaired a meeting at the urging of Jane Addams for Robert La Follette, and even while at Yale he had considered an offer to move to Washington as an assistant in the agricultural department. But his brush with the leadership of Detroit in the Interracial Committee involved him in political action and compromise with the Christian gospel, and those compromises continued throughout his life as he sought to live out the responsibility of a Christian ethic. His chairmanship of the Mayor's Committee was seldom mentioned by him, but he reflected the experience in his most brilliant essay on reforming race relations in 1968 in which he reflected on the Kerner Commission's report on violence, politics, and race. These reports on the commissions began and ended his work on race, but many of his critics have not noticed one or the other.[12]

The leaders of his congregation in the late 1920s learned they had to share him with the larger world. His charismatic brilliance led to speaking opportunities in colleges around the country, and his organizational skills led beyond service to his church as advisor to the Evangelical Synod chaplains, in World War I and then to St. Louis as a denominational-ecumenical leader, and even beyond to New York City to represent his denomination. This Mayor's Commission on race represented what became his third priority, rivaling his work in labor economics.[13] One summer his brother Helmut Richard Niebuhr filled in at Bethel, and then the Synod furnished him with an assistant who held the church together with his mother. Yet when he was in town he led the youth classes and the Boy Scouts as any small town pastor might have. Sometimes

---

11. Niebuhr, *Man's Nature*, 17–18.

12. An example of this type of critic is referred to in my letter "Niebuhr's Record on Race," 7. Even a careful Niebuhr scholar such as James Cone does not record that he read either of the reports on race in Detroit. See Cone, *Cross and the Lynching Tree*, 10–64.

13. Niebuhr, "Negro in Detroit."

he was only in town for a couple of days per week, and when required the congregation would release him for his ten-week trips to Europe where he was immersed in European lectures and interviews with leading government or ecclesiastical representatives. His development as a national leader pulled him away gradually from his successful ministry. He refused offers of academic and journalistic positions until Sherwood Eddy led him to an editorship and academic post in New York at the *World Tomorrow* and Union Theological Seminary in 1928.

4. Bethel Church Dispute

FOUR BLACK FAMILIES SPORADICALLY attended Bethel Evangelical Church under Niebuhr's leadership. Apparently their own congregations in the black churches persuaded them to retain their memberships. The issue of black membership arose and Niebuhr's successor, Adelbert Heim, took a strong position for their membership. Niebuhr incautiously at first criticized him for his radical and judgmental stand on the issue. After dismissing him as minister, the church council tried to recall him, but the congregation would not approve him by the two-thirds vote necessary. Later the council voted for a new rule to exclude black people from membership. That formal vote to exclude black people aroused Niebuhr's wrath and he wrote a letter distancing himself form the church's action and raised the question of the adequacy of his ministry on the subject.[1]

His first reaction was that he thought to resign from the congregation. On further reflection, he decided to remain, and that he could not repudiate the church as it revealed the inadequacy of his own ministry. "I have always believed that race prejudice is one of the most serious evils in our day with which the Christian gospel must deal."[2] While he did not expect many blacks to join Bethel, he regarded ruling against black membership as apostasy. It weakened the church morally and it made the mission movement of the church a travesty. Fanning racial prejudice into a hot

---

1. Niebuhr, "Church Council."
2. Niebuhr, "Church Council," 1.

flame was a most unchristian response to the dispute within the congregation. He called for the church to reconsider its action. He doubted if he would ever preach in the church again, and he questioned if whether, after his letter, they would ever ask him to return to preach. He admitted he was still confused, but that he would remain a member to bear the shame of their action. The concluding sentence was admitting that every anti-Christian journal in the Eastern world could use the action to prove that Christians never really believed in the lord of love.[3]

---

3. Niebuhr, "Church Council."

5. Moral Man and Immoral Society

NIEBUHR WAS WELCOMED TO New York and to the joint editorship of *The World Tomorrow* with the recognition of having chaired the Mayor's Committee on Race Relations in Detroit. He referenced the experience indirectly in his 1932 publication *Moral Man and Immoral Society: A Study in Ethics and Politics,* when he commented that governmental commissions on race could accomplish some improvements in race relations, but they were limited because they presupposed the limits of the community in improving the fate of the minority.[1] The book was not a theological text, but a rational or philosophic examination of the relationship between ethics and politics. Religion first appeared in the book at about page 50, and while the discussion was mostly about the religious consciousness of the United States, it referred a little to other religions. It tried to avoid claiming the authority of Christian symbols, but he was only three years away from directing the Bethel Evangelical Church. The study recognized that while ideals have influence in moving society, secularism, and technology had reduced the influence of religious ideals. He suspended the narrative between the dialogue of idealism with which he associated the social gospel and the realism of his Detroit experience in war, racism, and capitalist economics. He found the Marxist critique of Western capitalism to be more realistic than the Christian defense of the Western world. While he still wrote for the *Christian Century* his commitments

---

1. Niebuhr, *Moral Man*, 253.

were now to the socialist journal *The World Tomorrow*. The movement is best understood as a move from the liberal wing of the social gospel movement to the Marxist side of the social gospel. The book itself is not understood unless the Marxist interpretation of the social gospel is credited. Additionally, he moved away from the pacifism and prohibition aspects of the social gospel to a more realist reading of American society. These changes shocked the readership he had developed in his *Christian Century* following.

While references about improvements for black people appear scattered throughout the book, the major discussion of overcoming racism appears in the chapter, "The Preservation of Moral Values in Politics." The chapter stresses the effectiveness of continuing moral values even when force is being used to change society. Niebuhr regarded Gandhi very highly, and had hoped to spend time in India studying his methods. While arguing with some of his definitions regarding nonresistance and nonviolent resistance, Niebuhr celebrated his work.

Nonviolent resistance was particularly useful for a minority group that could not succeed using violence. It was not an absolute, but a method for some situations. Drawing upon Gandhi, he suggested:

> The emancipation of the Negro race in America probably waits upon the adequate development of this kind of social and political strategy. It is hopeless for the Negro to expect complete emancipation from the menial social and economic position into which the white man has forced him, merely by trusting in the moral sense of the white race. It is equally impossible to hope for emancipation through violent rebellion.[2]

Neither education nor commissions can persuade the white race to grant justice to blacks; only power can win freedom for the minority. The use of armed force, though, would only lead to catastrophe. Boycotts and in some cases nonpayment of taxes suggested hope for black people. Early in his work in New York he

---

2. Niebuhr, *Moral Man*, 252.

5. MORAL MAN AND IMMORAL SOCIETY

tried to explain to a group of black ministers why boycotts were an effective tool for the church to use to strive for racial justice.[3]

The recognition of religious values in promoting nonviolent resistance to evil was not immediately available in the Western world. An Eastern perspective like Gandhi's found it an easier achievement. "The white man is a fiercer beast of prey than the oriental."[4] Niebuhr, at the time, could not have imagined a revitalized black church leading the movement. Three decades later young white students would flock to seminaries to follow church leadership in the struggle for justice. Martin Luther King Jr. would read Niebuhr two decades later in seminary and would write academic papers in which Niebuhr's social pessimism seemed a little too dark. Later he would use Niebuhr and Gandhi for his own emancipation movement. Niebuhr had a lot to learn from the black church, as King drew upon Niebuhr. King would become more realistic but he would not divide personal and social ethics so sharply. Niebuhr needed the division to understand his own mind on race, but even more so he felt the need to denounce the ineffectiveness of the white church and government on race while admitting many nice individuals were no help on structural racial issues. Both Niebuhr and King would evolve and change and I wish they had met, as I wish James Cone and Niebuhr could have met. Throughout this definitive volume, *Moral Man and Immoral Society*, which Niebuhr wrote in a hurry as he was getting married, he tried to hold religious ideals and realism together in social strategy. Later he would understand religion was not quite so idealistic and Marxism was not so true as he imagined it to be in 1932–34. I noticed as one hundred seminarians prepared to submit to jail in Washington, DC, after protesting the Vietnam War that there were more copies of *Moral Man and Immoral Society* left in the church where we slept than any other book. Some students were among the more idealistic and some among the realists, and a few understood how the book was a synthesis. So was their war resistance.

---

3. Niebuhr, lecture on March 1, 1960, at Union Theological Seminary.
4. Niebuhr, *Moral Man*, 255.

Niebuhr saw how the privileged, for the most part, could not see the reality of their oppressive lifestyles and politics. Most of the argument of the book is for the guidance of the workers' revolt, he understood the anger and rage of the proletariat as he would understand James Cone's anger sixty years later, when he approved of his admittance to the Union faculty. In the 1930s he still wrote more about the needs of the white proletariat than he focused on black people, and that was from a perspective formulated in a white society rather than a black one. Racism was the work of white civilization and from his whole philosophy he could muster empathy, but not identity, with the victims.

6. Building Institutions in the South

WHILE WRITING *MORAL MAN and Immoral Society* and courting Ursula, one of his students drew him into another project that would impact the world of race relations in dramatic ways. The story is best recorded in Myles Horton's autobiography *The Long Haul*.[1] Horton came to Union from the mountains of Tennessee without a strong academic background. He was one of four Southerners at the school, all of whom were a little in awe of the well-educated Northerners from fine colleges. He found the friendliness of the young Reinhold Niebuhr to be a big help to him. He explained that most of the students addressed him as Reinie and that Reinie invited him to join a graduate seminar. After the first day the student failed to understand what the professor was talking about. He tried a second day, but during the break he told Niebuhr that he was not coming back because he could not understand anything he said. He advised Niebuhr that he would go to the library and use the time for reading. Niebuhr insisted that Horton understood despite his denials. He then asked the other gathering students whether they understood him. They said they did not understand either. Niebuhr said something was wrong and he insisted Horton stay in the class to keep him honest. Horton reported that Niebuhr would sometimes interrupt the class to ask Horton whether he understood.

Horton soaked up New York City's various worship opportunities and learned about social action. He went to rallies, strikes,

---

1. Horton, *Long Haul*.

and labor organizing meetings. He was asked to leaflet for an International Ladies Garment Workers Union strike. He was promised union assistance if he were arrested. His hands were cold and he was warned not to litter or to stand in the street. He developed a method of shoving the leaflets out from under his sleeve. The cop told him he could not do that there. Horton smiled and said:

> Oh yeah, you can hand them out anywhere if you're careful, but you've got to be very careful not to litter, it's against the law to litter. You've got to hold them tight so you do not drop any of them, and all the time I kept giving them out. See, you hold them this way and push them out.[2]

He played his little song and dance for the second cop who came over to tell him he could not hand them out, and eventually, to his amazement, they left him alone and he leafleted all day. He joined other demonstrations, learned about unions and became radicalized. With Niebuhr and Harry Ward's encouragement he went to Denmark to study labor relations and the cooperative movement.

On his return, he was more determined than ever; to return to the mountains and start a school there to inform people about social causes, unionization, and progressive social change.

Niebuhr persuaded his patron, Sherwood Eddy, to give Horton the first one hundred dollars to initiate the Highlander School in Tennessee. He used the mailing list from the treasurer of *World Tomorrow* to send out a fundraising letter signed by his allies from the journal. In part, Niebuhr wrote:

> May 27, 1932
> We are writing you in behalf of an educational project which we believe merits the support of all who are interested in more effective labor leadership and action. Our project is the organization of a Southern Mountains School for the training of labor leaders in the southern industrial areas. The southern mountaineers who are being drawn into the coal and textile industries are

---

2. Horton, *Long Haul*, 61.

6. Building Institutions in the South

completely lacking in understanding the problems of industry and the necessities of labor organization. We believe that neither A. F. of L. nor Communist leadership is adequate to their needs. Our hope is to train the radical leaders who will understand the need of both political and union strategy. Without local leadership a labor movement in the South is impossible. The need for such leadership becomes more urgent when it is realized that the individualistic outlook of the mountain people makes it hard for them to understand or accept leadership from without.... We are proposing to use education as one of the instruments for bringing about a new social order. Assuming that an individual can be integrated by having his interest aroused in a great cause in which he can lose himself, our problems—individual integration, relation of the individual to a new situation, and education for a socialistic society—become one.[3]

Beyond raising funds, Niebuhr served on the advisory board of the school which became the Highlander Center in East Tennessee. In the 1950s the Highlander Center became focused on teaching nonviolent massive civil disobedience for integration of society. It was here that Rosa Parks, the heroine of the Montgomery bus boycott, received training and inspiration:

> I found out for the first time in my adult life that this could be a unified society, that there was such a thing as peoples of different races and backgrounds meeting together in workshops and living together in peace and harmony.[4]

Later, the center was vilified by segregationists who posted pictures of Martin Luther King Jr. among socialists at the center's twenty-fifth anniversary party on billboards and identified him as attending a "communist training school."[5] The importance of the Horton story for this book rests in Niebuhr's involvement in the South and his hopes to avoid alienation by involving people

3. Niebuhr, "Fundraising Letter."
4. Surratt, "Miles Horton," 399.
5. Surratt, "Miles Horton," 399.

in a great social movement. Throughout his life he was never far from investing his life in causes and finding his life's fulfillment in this giving, as he thought Jesus promised. Here also is the academic acting and urging others to act. Coincidentally, some of the civil rights movement seems to have started here in training in nonviolence, which based in Gandhi's teaching and was Niebuhr's preferred method for winning black empowerment. Academic evaluations of Niebuhr on race, which are not based in social action, as well as reading are not likely to produce an adequate picture of Niebuhr on race relations. The correlation of his positions in *Moral Man and Immoral Society*, including a priority at the beginning of the New Deal on organizing labor, needs to be recognized for interpreters of Niebuhr. Organized labor was a major component, as recorded here, for social change.

His writing in 1933 was more on the depression, Roosevelt, Jews, and the foreboding international situation, than it was on race relations. However, his passion for reflecting on the role of social action in changing race relations is seen in his note in the *World Tomorrow*[6] on the NAACP action against Kroger stores in Toledo. Here they won rights to employment through the use of economic boycott. Blacks had to find levers of power. Refusing to buy where they could not work was a major tool in empowerment. Church participation was a factor and it made clear how Christian ethics needed to include economic pressure to correct the basic injustices against black people.

While courting Ursula Keppel-Compton, the English Fellow that year, he was also teaching and interacting with the German Fellow, Dietrich Bonhoeffer. Bonhoeffer thought at the time that Niebuhr's work was too political, but as he became politically active in Germany he became more appreciative of Niebuhr's activism. One of the stranger interpretations of Niebuhr and Bonhoeffer is to praise Bonhoeffer for reading works by black authors while criticizing the professor who assigned those works in his course on religion and literature.[7] In Niebuhr's course, Bonhoeffer read

---

6. Niebuhr, "Ex Cathedra," 2.

7. Cone, *Cross and the Lynching Tree*, 42.

6. Building Institutions in the South

W. E. B. Dubois, A. Locke, C. Cullen, B. T. Washington, and L. Hughes. Bonhoeffer involved himself in the Abyssinian Church in Harlem, and in deep involvement in black culture in his academic year at Union. The tragic developments of 1933–45 blocked the further development of these issues.

The World Tomorrow suspended publication in 1934, and Niebuhr left the Fellowship of Reconciliation the same year. He founded *Radical Religion* the next year as the journal for the Fellowship of Socialist Christians. In its first issue Niebuhr's editorial defended Angelo Herman, a black activist who was sentenced on false charges to twenty years on a chain gang whereas most on the chain gangs could not live ten years. Niebuhr pleaded for support of him from all social activists. He was skeptical of ministers rallying to Herman's cause because of his communist affiliations.

The most fascinating essay in the third issue of *Radical Religion* was Sherwood Eddy's report of his visit to the Tenant Farmers Union. He found tenant farmers being evicted and lynched when they protested against working conditions in the South. He and Sam Franklin were imprisoned and threatened with death. The attempts to unionize resulted in evictions and/or unemployment. Eddy hit upon the idea of a cooperative farm and paid the down payment for a farm in the Mississippi Delta. Sam Franklin assumed the chores of leading the farm, which soon grew to thirty-three families living cooperatively in an integrated society. Eventually a second farm, Providence, was secured. Eddy carried the story of the farm to the secretary of agriculture, Henry Wallace, and to Mrs. Eleanor Roosevelt, and won their support.

Eddy's support for an integrated cooperative resulted in an appeal for funds, and the Delta Cooperative Farm was started. Sam Franklin, who had come to study with Niebuhr, became its executive director, and it involved Niebuhr deeply as chair of the board and in sharing his social philosophy for several years. Its early tenants were refugees from white farms who lost their homes and roles for supporting unionization of rural labor. For Franklin these tenants moved from conditions of semi-slavery to citizenship on the farm. Franklin regarded his strategy in Niebuhr's terms of announcing absolute ideals, respecting the limits of the society, and achieving limited victories. Among the moving paragraphs of Franklin's description of the project was the recognition of the beauty of integrated worship with this displaced rural proletariat.

The farm suffered from floods, fires, the Depression, and other problems of rural life over the years, and Niebuhr had to work on the economics of the farm. He presided over a particularly difficult board meeting in 1939. The management of the farm by a distant board presented its own set of problems, and Niebuhr complained about having to go to Mississippi again while also regarding it as one of the most successful strategies of Christian social action at the time. The addition of the Providence Farm complicated the management of the two as one unit. And the Delta Farm was governed by the Providence Farm when Sam Franklin went off to serve in World War II.

Niebuhr reported in 1938 on the two farms that received grants from The Fellowship of Socialist Christians. The investment in the farms was reported at about $100,000, and Niebuhr was appealing for another $10,000. "The task of building a cooperative venture within the terribly depressed economy of the South is a very difficult one."[8] The same essay mentioned the initiation of the school for black ministers at the farm. Earlier essays had Niebuhr commenting on the farm's losses to the depressed price of cotton, and how the new farm one hundred miles away at Providence would be diversified in crops and animals. He found the morale on the place to be higher in 1938 than preciously and he projected a hopeful but difficult future. Racism defeated the first farm when four boys from the farm were charged with harassing a white girl, whereas the real problem was the integration features of the farm.

The farm, Providence, continued until threats from the White Citizens' Council closed it in 1955 with charges of communism and integration. Niebuhr responded in *Christianity and Crisis* claiming the White Citizens' Council was little better than the Ku Klux Klan. Franklin regarded the persecution of the farms as part of the backlash against the Supreme Court's decision in 1954 to

---

8. Niebuhr, "Delta Cooperative Farm," 7.

6. Building Institutions in the South

integrate the schools. The farm's existence for a score of years in an integrated-cooperative manner is part of the story of Niebuhr in race relations. He knew his participation in the South was ambivalent. He met so much suffering and he accomplished so little.

> I have a passion for alleviating race and group prejudice. But I don't know how much of my activity satisfies my own pride. At any rate my love hasn't gone far enough to persuade me to identify with any minority group and share its difficulties.[9]

He knew he could not walk in the shoes of either the Detroit newcomers or the black proletarian farmers of the South. He met with Southern ministers who disapproved of the Delta Farm and regarded him as a Yankee interloper. He appreciated their hostility, but he persisted with the farm. Their defense of "Southern customs" seemed hollow to him as on the train back north he read of the Southern custom of lynching.[10] He knew the condemnation of the South was too simple, he had guided the report on race in Detroit. He saw potential in the poor blacks of the South rising up if they could get organized. Maybe a renewal of the church there would provide hope. After a meeting of the Tenant Farmers Union, he said it was the first time he had seen a union meeting opening with prayer. The labor speakers knew how to use the relevant scriptural passages to inspire their listeners. There was a "high degree of potency" in that simple Southern religion of black people.[11] However, he knew that many of the spectators of the hanging of the two black boys were Christians. One choked to death as the trap door misfired, and Christian criticism of the gallows and the churches was silent. For Niebuhr, if the church failed on the racial atrocities it was broken.

The failure of the church was so obvious and Niebuhr doubted his own adequacy. He was close to despair as he reflected on

---

9. Niebuhr, "Why I Am Not a Christian," 1482.
10. Niebuhr, "Meditations from Mississippi," 183–84.
11. Niebuhr, "Meditations from Mississippi," 183.

his own work in Detroit.[12] He recognized the near universality of racial prejudice, but it was particularly rabid among his own Nordic European population. In the North, "The housing situation is the crux of the race problem in every city."[13] By Niebuhr's criteria of 1927, and the realities of the housing situation in 2024, the whole validity of the Christian faith is in doubt. The police killing of African Americans has continued, and the killing of youth by black youth is shameful. In Detroit there were twenty-four police shootings of black people in 1926 without any investigations of police.[14] Today there are more murders and more investigations.

The decade of 1926–37 may have been Niebuhr's most active in race relations. *The World Tomorrow* had described their new editor in 1928 as an expert in race relations, economy, and international relations. The drift into World War II found Niebuhr emphasizing collective security, international relations and organizations, preventing war, and the saving of Jews, more than black-white relations. At the end of the decade, he was writing his theology. Race relations provided a crisis in his own thinking, human nature had been proven less innocent than the country expected, and the pre-war theology reflected that stubborn reality. His half-a-dozen essays on race reflect his discouragement on improving race relations or overcoming black poverty, and without the power of property, freedom was mostly a sham. It is now hard to analyze his neighborhood relations. He has one reference of early discussions with black leaders in Harlem and his attempts to persuade them that economic boycotts were one of the effective tools for achieving more racial justice.[15] He had conversations with ministers about starting an interracial church, but according to Professors Bennett and Shinn the black pastors were reluctant to surrender the members who could be interested in such a move.[16]

---

12. Niebuhr, "Race Prejudice in the North," 583–84.

13 Niebuhr, "Race Prejudice in the North," 583.

14. Niebuhr, "Race Prejudice in the North," 583.

15 Niebuhr, "Lecture in History of Christian Ethics," Union Theological Seminary, March 1, 1960.

16 Conversations with John C. Bennett and Roger L. Shinn, 1967–68.

6. Building Institutions in the South

One other anecdote was a black professor criticizing Donald McCann's book on liberation theology and Niebuhr at a Society of Christian Ethics meeting for not including references to Niebuhr's many meetings with black pastors in New York City. In 1937 and 1938, Niebuhr got down into the real weeds of racial justice as he published the details of the Delta Farm board meetings in *Radical Religion*.[17] Those who think he remained at too abstract a level or too theological a level need to read Niebuhr on tractors and sweet potatoes.

Niebuhr knew that his project for cooperatives and reform arose out of the mixed traditions of liberalism and Marxism that operated in his mind. The Christian church had assumed the Stoic ideal of human equality for life in the church and some Christians freed their slaves. But the mixture of obedience to social structures including government and slavery became dominant. Social equality was present in the kingdom of God, but for most of Christian history slavery was tolerated. Niebuhr, with his high regard for the pessimistic reading of Christian ethics from Ernst Troeltsch, turned toward other social sources for political theory, and in 1934 he expressed it as needing a radical social theory and a conservative or orthodox theology expressed symbolically. For most of Christianity social rules were divine ordinances. Piety urged one to accept slavery. He noted Calvinism had a tradition of resistance and revolution to heretical rule or rules.[18] But the ethical social resources he needed came from American liberalism grounded in the enlightenment or Marxism. He read the radical ethics of Jesus as convicting his own efforts as inadequate. In the last year of his life he wrote to me dismissing this book, *Reflections on the End of an Era,* as too Marxist. He regarded the ethos of the discriminating South as a mixture of American individualism, religious sentimentalism, and pious respect for the status quo institutions, and power hungry, capitalist privilege by the ruling class there. He also believed that the ethos would change only slowly through repeated pressure. Governmental decisions would be overruled by the ethos

17. Niebuhr, "Delta Cooperative Farm."
18. Niebuhr, *Reflections on the End*, 218–22.

as had prohibition. Liberal church positions on race were denied by the church's segregated status. The difficulties of achieving fairness even today in housing and education, regarded as major issues by "The Negro in Detroit," substantially point toward his wisdom on the issue.

Before concluding this section on building institutions in the South, and moving into his years of writing on race during World War II, it is warming to remember that he was speaking in the South during the 1930s and meeting both blacks and whites. We do not have a list of these talks, sermons, and lectures. He was a fundraiser, sometimes board chairman, and philosopher of the Highlander School and the Delta Farm, and those responsibilities always intersected with his Christian ethical work and perspective. His work, and the work of the Southern churches, was influenced by the social and financial realities of the 1930s. He participated with A. Philip Randolph, the head of the Pullman Porter's Union, in talking about unionization of the workers in the summer, and then went on to speak at two youth conferences, one white and one black. He found the conferences to be among the most significant developments in Christian conscience awakening. In the car between the conferences, one black girl told him of making a white friend in the other camp while serving as a fraternal visitor. Her mother doubted that the friendship could endure beyond the camp experience and refused to believe her daughter when she testified that her white friend was still friendly with her in her hometown. She told Niebuhr that she never lied to her mother, but that her mother could not believe the story of the warm relationship continuing even back home. In his later reflections Niebuhr praised the presence of black fraternal visitors to the white camp, but condemned the religious sanction for prejudice exhibited in the fact that the black delegates could not eat with the white youth. Niebuhr began his short essay welcoming the Southern hospitality of both black and white hospitality even within the segregated world. His appreciation of Southern charm was accompanied by his harsh criticism of segregation, which he regarded as a major factor in encouraging racial hatred, which if tolerated led to

6. Building Institutions in the South

lynchings by mob action.[19] He drew upon the earlier findings of the research on Detroit to critique race relations in the North and emphasized the segregation in housing as a fundamental breeding ground of racial contempt.[20]

In 1933, he criticized the churches for the quietism regarding anti-Semitism in regard to "the extravagances of the Nazi terror" against the Jews.[21] He detailed atrocities against the Jews including executions and called for a worldwide protest against the Nazis. He had little respect for the German churches and he did not want Christian sympathy for fellow Christians to dull the criticism. In 1934, *The World Tomorrow* folded, and Niebuhr's last essay was on the Fellowship of Socialist Christians, which he led. Another professor was moved into administration of the seminary so that Niebuhr could be given a chair in "applied Christianity." Yale University's pursuit of Niebuhr had moved President Coffin to provide a position commensurate with his rising reputation as a writer and analyst. Six months after the demise of *The World Tomorrow*, he founded *Radical Religion* to continue his Christian socialism. He kept searching for a way to create a leftist expression of Christianity that would be adequate to the times of depression when Europe was collapsing under fascism and Nazism. The late 1930s were dominated in his writing with his analysis of European politics and though he still wrote about racism, his focus was more on the suffering of the Jews and European politics. Not until 1936 did his critique of President Roosevelt lessen and though he had supported Thomas's campaign he voted for Roosevelt. He continued to hope for labor joining the socialist cause and he continued attacking Henry Ford's pretensions. His ministry at Bethel and his developing radicalism, still within the social gospel, had emerged during the growing disenchantment with Wilson and his three Republican successors. He voted for Norman Thomas in 1932, but for the mixed economy and international realism of Franklin D. Roosevelt in 1936.

19. Niebuhr, "Glimpses of the Southland."
20. Niebuhr, "Race Prejudice in the North."
21. Niebuhr, "Religion and the New Germany," 845.

Though he had been president of the Fellowship of Reconciliation he resigned as his hopes for peace no longer translated into its more total pacifism. He expressed his hopes for socialism in terms that could under certain conditions support violent defense of the workers and he hoped for collective security against the demonic tendencies of Europe. Pragmatism regarding violence now replaced Marxist certainty or Christian absolutism about violence.

7. Palestine-Israel

URSULA NIEBUHR BROUGHT HIS writing in *The Nation*[1] in 1942 to me. He recognized the reality of Judaism as a nation as well as a religion and he called for a national homeland, arguing for Palestine to be the homeland for Jews after the holocaust. It was within the discussion of American foreign policy and the British Empire. He urged the meeting of Arab claims and hoped economic benefits to the Arabs could be seen as partial compensation, though he recognized such a settlement was an injustice to the Arabs. This increase in militancy for Israel was reflected in his mid-1942 organization of the Christian Council on Palestine, which gathered three thousand pastors to support its Zionist position. When the official Anglo-American Committee held hearings in January, 1946, Niebuhr testified for a Jewish state in Palestine as well as for more openness for Jewish migration to Palestine. The final report of the committee largely agreed with Niebuhr, as did President Truman, but the commission referred the statement to the United Nations in 1947.

In 1944–45 he wrote about communism's prospects in Cuba, the Ethiopian War, the developments in Russia, and politics in France and Great Britain. But he also analyzed Southern congressmen and antilynching laws, which he supported. His brief

---

1. Niebuhr, "Jews After the War," 214–16, 253–55.

comments on lynching in *Radical Religion*[2] were followed by more substantial analysis of race issues in Mississippi.[3]

Niebuhr's wartime writing on the race problem contained the broader racial issues of the Japanese[4] in his new journal. His lectures on racism in the seminar I assisted him in during the late 1960s still combined his remarks on Judaism and black relations with more of an emphasis on the tensions and horrors between black and white. Though the seminar often included activists on the racial issues, the students in those years would try to divert him to the Vietnam War and international relations.

His writing on race during World War II also dealt with practical issues like black people and the railroads,[5] or the educational functions regarding race in the army,[6] to more theoretical issues like reflections on Gunnar Myrdal's *An American Dilemma.*[7] The FBI investigation of Niebuhr during the war picked up a notation that Niebuhr was part of the NAACP's Committee of 100, which was supporting a dinner address by Myrdal.[8]

Niebuhr's philosophy of social ethics and politics undergirded his writing on race relations, and produced themes for his actions and theories. It also influenced black writers and was crucial for both Martin Luther King Jr., and James Cone. The theological writings of 1941 did not discuss race relations except for a quick condemnation of slavery. But the statements on the ambiguity of politics, the unfinished nature of historical actions, and the role of power in the struggle for justice were a fundamental contribution to their theories of action. Volume Two of *The Nature and Destiny of Man*[9] was published in 1941, before the foolish bombing of Pearl

---

2. Niebuhr, "Brief Comments," 8–9.
3. Niebuhr, "Meditations from Mississippi," 183–84.
4. Niebuhr, "Race Problem," 3–5.
5. Niebuhr, "Negroes and the Railroads," 11.
6. Niebuhr, "Editorial Notes," 2.
7. Niebuhr, "Review of Gunnar Myrdal," 2.
8. Federal Bureau of Investigation investigation of Reinhold Niebuhr. Obtained under the Freedom of Information Act.
9. Niebuhr, *Moral Man.*

7. Palestine-Israel

Harbor brought the United States into the war. The lectures had been delivered in 1939 as the bombing began in Edinburgh.

The first few pages of chapter 10 summarize his philosophy of social ethics in its mature form. The chapter title, including the phrase "the Kingdom of God," reveals his social gospel origins, and the "struggle for social justice" presumes his Christian faith synthesizing with his realism. His friend John C. Bennett regarded it as his best chapter on social ethics. Communal life is meant to be improved, as humanity cannot find fulfillment outside of love in community. Love is the essence of human nature and justice is the essence of community life. Community life can be improved, but their will always be levels of corruption. Good and evil will continue to expand, and humanity's struggles for social justice and growth will be only partially fulfilled and often they will be frustrated. The dialectic of love and justice, which D. B. Robertson emphasized so well,[10] is not spoken of here, but it is the reality of the dialectical character of Christian social ethics. There would not be unambiguous policy on race. To win good legislation requires votes reflecting the egos of others' votes, which have to be pursued. Their were no politics without the implied use of force and compromise. My friend James Cone learned a lot from this chapter, and I heard him preach the best sermon on justice I have ever heard reflecting some of this chapter. However, I do not think he adequately learned the ambiguity of social change policies and actions. From my working in politics directly I have come to appreciate Niebuhr more and James less on these issues, and I hope we shared that difference adequately, frequently in his wonderful class on Niebuhr. Niebuhr learned from the installation of Saul that the King was a divine blessing, but also a human institution that would exact its toll from the people. But of course just as there is no one absolute standard of justice, the lack of justice evokes a greater price from blacks than it does from whites, and the rage of blacks is justified and whites have been too long in not correcting the practice of injustice in the society they control.

---

10. Robertson, *Love and Justice*.

The writing on the types of power sources recognizes both material and spiritual forces.[11] They usually interpenetrate each other. Fascism, communism, and Nazism expressed mixtures of spiritual, political, economic, and organizational power. Democracies have a different mixture. Racism involves mixtures of power including the spiritual. The overcoming of racism will require mixtures of power. Black people, in his estimation, during the war years lacked access to many of the instruments of power. In my estimation, those representing economic power in the United States were not self-inclined to challenge racism or white supremacy. The government had accepted slavery for much of its history, and denied equality for all its existence. The reality of black impatience for change had minor impact during the war years, though President Truman moved to integrate the army. Progress awaited particular developments for unleashing the black church and moral power with legal initiatives in the 1950s. Niebuhr often regarded the civil rights movement as stemming from a synthesis of despair and hope. He saw the government as more susceptible to moral or spiritual power than the other instruments of military and economic power. But the hopes laid dormant until a hero arose from the black church and academia. Maybe not every reader will find Niebuhr's framework for social change as easily available in this chapter as I have. Cone told me that underneath his first book *Black Power* was Niebuhr even though he quoted Karl Barth on whom he had just written a dissertation for Northwestern University. Niebuhr's dialogue criticizing Emil Brunner and Barth's inadequacies for American social ethics here reflects his social gospel inheritance.

---

11. Niebuhr, "Kingdom of God," 244–86.

8. Martin Luther King Jr.

NIEBUHR'S INFLUENCE IS REFLECTED in Rosa Parks, who was taught nonviolent resistance at the Highlander School and whose boldness ignited the movement led by Martin Luther King Jr. in Montgomery. King studied with Niebuhr in seminary and he did not always agree with him. Niebuhr both criticized and praised King. Andrew Young, King's disciple and collaborator, expressed King's use of Niebuhr as forcefully as anyone:

> I want to begin by saying that there was always a misunderstanding of what Martin Luther King was about. I remember one night when someone came at him with some of the strict presuppositions of Ghandian nonviolence. And he responded about three o'clock in the morning with the most brilliant lecture I have ever heard on *The Nature and Destiny of Man,* Reinhold Niebuhr, the thinking of John Bennett, and *Christianity and Crisis.* He reminded us that he had done his PhD thesis on Paul Tillich, and you realized how everything he did was formulated more out of a sense of Christian realism and the Black reality of the Christian church in the southern part of the Untied States, than I think the press ever really understood.
>
> We always tried to make nonviolence something that was very spiritual and ethereal for the saints to live by, and never really understood as something Dr. Niebuhr said as far back as *Moral Man and Immoral Society,* that nonviolent power and economic withdrawal would be

the means that the Black community might eventually use to gain justice.[1]

Niebuhr came to recognize King as the most effective Protestant. He supported King in print after King's speech at Riverside Church opposing the Vietnam War. Often their rhetoric sounded similar, with both of them condemning the government's turning away from support for welfare legislation to fund the war. They sometimes differed in priorities but their goals for justice were very similar. King was usually more optimistic than Niebuhr in his rhetoric, but he also knew how tough the road toward racial justice was. Niebuhr has been criticized for not joining King in marches, but he could hardly walk. King came to join the organization Clergy and Laity Concerned about Vietnam and it supported his speaking at Riverside Church. Niebuhr supported King's nonviolent campaigns as against his more militant black critics. For Niebuhr the advocating of violence for an unarmed minority made no strategic sense. King had criticized Niebuhr in the student papers he had written for not appreciating enough the power of the gospel for change. Niebuhr wanted King in his campaigns to become a little more realistic. Events forced realism on King as he conducted his later campaigns. They learned from each other. Niebuhr came to appreciate the spirit and the power of black churches and nonviolent campaigns produced more power than Niebuhr's earlier understandings. King learned from the realism of *Moral Man and Immoral Society*, and they both learned from Gandhi.

---

1. Young, "Speech at Testimonial Dinner," 80.

9. Realism and Idealism

WORLD WAR II DREW toward a close. Niebuhr wrote a lot about the dangers of the pride of victors,

> European and World politics, increasing tensions with Russia, the United Nations and in 1945 one essay about race. It was a very theological piece on the inadequacies of science on the race question. Racial malevolence was so drastic that it took more than learning to combat it. It required repentance and the overcoming of pride. The church had its own resources in repentance and forgiveness, and in the theological understanding of human pride. Racial conflict was the most serious problem the nation faced after the war and according to Niebuhr it would get worse before it became better. "The sins that the white man has committed against the colored man cry to heaven." He was not so appreciative of the church's attempt to tell the nation of its sin. He suggested that the church's mission might be better developed in building Christians who were truly repentant of the bigotry of racism.[1]

After this theological paper on race, his written emphasis on the problem dropped off in the 1940s and early 1950s. Between the essay above and "Justice to the American Negro from State, Community, and Church"[2] in 1956, Robertson's bibliography only records eight short pieces. These years were among his most

---

1. Niebuhr, "Christian Faith," 21–24.
2. Robertson, *Reinhold Niebuhr's Works*.

productive, covering the atomic technology, the United Nations, American foreign policy, Israel, politics, and a variety of religious subjects. The fifty pages of bibliography cover an estimated one thousand essays. It is no wonder that the important collection on his thought, edited by Charles Kegley and Robert Bretall,[3] at the end of the decade had no essay on Niebuhr on race. The early biography by June Bingham[4] only contains a few paragraphs about him and Martin Luther King Jr. and the later volume by Gordon Holland notes Niebuhr regarded it as the most important domestic problem, but wrote only briefly about the subject.[5] None of these sources explored in depth the Delta Farm, the Highlander School, or the Fellowship of Socialist Christians support for the Southern Tenant Farmers Organization. The 360-page collection by Davis and Good gave only ten pages to Niebuhr on race relations. These lacunae reflected how Niebuhr's work on race had relaxed. However, a strong essay locating racism in religious failure appeared in 1948.[6]

Niebuhr was discouraged in 1948. Racism was not in retreat, and he penned an essay predicting Truman's defeat by Thomas Dewey. His young admirer Hubert H. Humphrey, the mayor of Detroit, challenged the Democratic establishment speaking strongly on race, and advocating a strong plank on racial justice for the party. He prevailed at the convention and began the process of disentangling the South from its Democratic dominance. Many of the Southern delegates left the convention and the Dixiecrat party was formed to challenge President Truman. The coalition formed by Franklin D. Roosevelt was destroyed. Racial superiority for Niebuhr was seen in the almost universal human experience of valuing one's own values, experience, and culture as the highest good. Other virtues of people are devalued and punitive discrimination appears in the dominant group. He noted that

3. The revised version includes my essay with ten pages on the subject, Stone, "Contribution of Reinhold Niebuhr."
4. Bingham, *Courage to Change*, 110–11.
5. Harland, *Thought*, 255–71.
6 Niebuhr, "Sin of Racial Prejudice," 6.

9. Realism and Idealism

students in 1948 appeared less interested in economic injustice than the previous generation of students. He was still active in the several organizations that dealt with race, and he served as the presidential-appointed UNESCO delegate in Geneva. He wrote Ursula from Paris that he was told he occupied the suite that Hitler had used, but he was doubtful of the ascription. Three of the essays mentioned concerned South Africa's apartheid, essays on the Supreme Court and desegregation of schools, and a more major one on the failure of the Fair Employment Act in the Senate. He would recommend that the New Deal actions on lynching and the poll tax would have had a better chance of passing with perhaps some support from Southern senators. His production on race heated up in the later 1950s and my survey includes thirty-six pieces on race relations by the end of the decade. Several of these are short editorials in his own journals, but there are more major essays on black-white relations in the *New Leader*.

An essay that still is relevant today as we continue to struggle with the desegregation of schools was published in 1954. Niebuhr celebrated the school decision of 1954 as cheerful news in a season of "sorry realities and dread possibilities."[7] He was hopeful of its acceptance in both North and South, and he praised the statesmanship, recognizing the need for time for the decision to be implemented. He traced the history of the court from 1896 and the time it took for the 1954 decision. Social history recorded the distance between the ideal of equality and the realities of public acceptance of the ideal. I think Niebuhr's realism was more optimistic than the subsequent reality. Public schools still remain segregated in the South and the North. Our partially integrated neighborhood sees the busses bring the black students into the still segregated school while white students flee to charter or Catholic schools. Niebuhr received criticism for recognizing the slowness of progress toward equality between the races, and for his recognition of the appropriateness of the 1896 decision for its time. For him, however, the tension between ideals and reality was true to life. "Thus the Court wrote a great state paper as well as rendering

---

7. Niebuhr, "Supreme Court," 148.

a wise decision." Niebuhr saw progress in race relations, but there was a long struggle ahead.[8]

Two years later he endorsed the bus boycott at the beginning of Martin Luther King Jr.'s civil rights career and the need for changing the old tradition of segregation on buses. He regarded the boycott as a method of justice and not, as King might have said, a movement of love. His *Christianity and Society* editorial of spring 1956 celebrated the bus boycott in Montgomery that was in progress.[9] He commented that everyone should be heartened by the success of the pacifist organization.

The same year he responded to a Southern churchman regarding his fear of miscegenation if the barriers of segregation were dropped. He spoke of the common grace which was reducing segregation even if athletics seemed to be ahead of the church in overcoming segregation. He reminded the segregationist that there was nothing in the gospel demanding the defense of Southern culture or the American way of life. The gospel ethic was to love the neighbor and that customs that defied that ethic needed to be replaced. In another case he reminded his critic that the greatest extent of biracial sexual relations was during the time of slavery. In later years he would tell his class that love between blacks and whites contributed to overcoming bad relations between the races. In the 1956 essay, recognized evils were "dismantled by gradual, collective erosion. . . . But we must remember that racial arrogance has been the besetting sin of the white man which has made his conduct odious throughout the world."[10]

He cautioned against Northern self-righteous moralism. But he called for prudence as well as idealism. His words about sympathy for parents unable to accept integrated schools failed to achieve the rigor he recognized in Christian ideals even if it foretold the difficulty of integrating American schools or housing. Niebuhr recognized how separation encouraged the human tendencies toward pride and arrogance. He often dealt with the particulars of

---

8. Niebuhr, "Supreme Court."
9. Niebuhr, "Way of Non-violent Resistance," 3.
10. Niebuhr, "If Races 'Mix,'" 17–18.

9. Realism and Idealism

housing, education, or bussing, but at a deeper level he regarded racism as original sin or the human tendency toward idolatry of one's own group. He wanted the church to ally with anthropology and psychology but thought that its major contribution would be in increasing the number of contrite enlightened souls who would join in the practical fight against racial segregation. The same year he revisited the Supreme Court decision that separate facilities could never be equal. In fact the racist folks in the South never wanted the schools or education to be equal. Though he might have wanted slower changes in the school situation he understood that counsels of prudence would not be acceptable to black people. Counsels of slowness, though they may be prudent, would be dismissed as "ignoble compromise." "Furthermore, the effort of the racists to defy and circumvent the decision has given some southern states the quality of quasi Fascist terror and intimidation."[11]

He understood that the Supreme Court to an extent followed the election returns and adjusted slowly to changes in society. Local communities continued to resist the law. He hoped that the defiance of the law would gradually be overcome, but our continued experience showed that resistance to school integration or housing integration continues. The law as in this case can provide a creative role, but justice awaits changes in the community's perception of morality and human rights.[12] The Protestant church's resistance to justice in race relations was partially due to its "chumminess" while the greater Roman Catholic results in integration were partially due to its hierarchical role, which could enforce to an extent its morality. He regarded both Judaism and Catholicism as superior to Protestantism in advancing justice in race relations. Racial justice had to be advanced both from above and below, and Protestant churches usually lacked power from above. Democracy could not achieve justice when the local communities failed to want it. Even justice in voting had to wait until finally the country, with Johnson's presidency and the black fight for suffrage, could produce significant gains, which today some forces are attempting

11. Niebuhr, "Desegregation Issue," 3–4.
12. Niebuhr, "Justice to the American Negro," 129–44.

to thwart. Only recently I secured our church steps and clergy support for a rally press conference supporting voting rights.

10. Jews and Christians

NIEBUHR'S RECOGNITION THAT GROUP pride served to bond societies together and to strengthen order made the appearance of group pride or racism almost inevitable in human history. That frankness underlay his presentation to the joint faculty meeting between Jewish Theological Seminary and Union Theological Seminary, which was later published.[1] The tensions between Judaism and Christianity were not fated to disappear. Only a mature tolerance between the two could keep the peace. Majorities tended to oppress minorities and peace demanded overtures to reduce the stress.

The acceptance of the differences between Christians and Jews in the various Christian majority countries in which Jews lived were not primarily due to religion but they often took on religious flavoring. The communities embraced similar loyalties to their ultimate references and they shared some of the same scriptures. The rise of Christianity in ethnically gentile and Jewish communal loyalties led, in Niebuhr's judgment, to a variety of ethnic directions. So their respective tensions were ethnically and religiously influenced. Antisemitism was basically a human problem rather than a particularly Christian problem. The Jew was an offense to the Christian because he was his own ethnic and religious type, which differed from the majority in which they existed.

A mature toleration required recognition that both Christianity and Judaism were going to persevere. They each had their

---

1. Niebuhr, *Pious and Secular America*.

own integrity. Niebuhr did not, to my knowledge, explore deeply how anti-Judaism in the church reflected the struggle between early Christianity and the Judaism of the Roman Empire reflected in Christian Scripture. The bitterness of the early Christians is in the text.[2]

Christianity needed the justice of the prophets of Israel because the *agape* of the *New Testament* was inadequate for Christian social ethics. It was too ultimate and in bourgeois society it often drifted into sentimentality and became irrelevant. Niebuhr's talk on prophetic justice recognized the need to empower the poor to move toward justice and to guarantee charity for the disempowered. The ethics of the prophets were directly relevant to a society when order required corrective power to achieve justice.

Even the minority situation of the Jew allowed him to stand a little outside of the community as a critic. The Jew could see the suffering of black people, and seek justice for the minority. He often commented on the superiority of the Jewish community over the Christian in responding to the injustice of black people.

He found the commonality of these two faiths of Western civilization not only in monotheism, but in the common perspectives on the meaning of history and struggle for social righteousness seen in the prophets. They both found relative meaning first in the consciousness of the Hebrew people and then in the redemption of humanity in Jesus. But from these presuppositions two different faiths emerge, both founded in different covenants. The younger Christian faith rebelled in part against the elder tradition and claimed its own form of universalism.

In his own theological analysis of the faiths he developed three areas in which he found commonalities with different interpretations. Judaism and Christianity shared the issues of Messianism, grace and law, and the problems of particularity and universality. In all three they share symbolism with different interpretations. Niebuhr's favorite phrase for the difference came from Martin Buber: "To the Christian, the Jew is the stubborn fellow who is still waiting for the Messiah; to the Jew the Christian is the heedless

---

2. See Minear, "My Peace."

10. JEWS AND CHRISTIANS

fellow who in an unredeemed world declares that redemption has somehow or other taken place."[3]

Niebuhr was thankful for the sabbatical in 1958 at the Institute for Advanced Study. His study was how the perennial factors of national interaction were relevant to the complex modern issue of managing the nuclear competition between the Soviet Union and the United States. In examining the relations among French, Spanish, and English imperialism, he noted that British imperialism seemed to be less tolerant of native populations than French or Spanish. The Puritans were less likely than the French or Spanish to intermarry with indigenous populations and more prone to murder them. His four pages on the subject were not based on scholarly research, but rather ad hoc or commonsense generalizations.[4] He regarded British racism as a little less odious than the Dutch or German, but much worse than the policies of the more Latin-based nations. There was nothing in the pages to make imperialist racism any more moral than the general pursuit of power in international relations that had pretensions of moral purpose, but really reflected the human sin of international politics in an immoral system. The white reviewers, mostly experts in international reviews, did not comment on those four pages. Herbert Edwards commented on the pages in his critique of Niebuhr in the post-Niebuhr *Christianity and Crisis* of 1987.[5] Unfortunately he followed Richard Fox in dismissing Niebuhr's commitment to writing about civil rights and he ignored his practical actions for racial justice. Edwards's real fight with Niebuhr was with Niebuhr's stressing the reality of evil that continued alongside and sometimes within the Christian movement. Niebuhr in race relations, as in other human endeavors, conceded more to evil than Edwards chose to see. Even in Edwards's larger piece where he criticized "Christian realism" in general, he failed to note Niebuhr's major actions against racism or to read his major writings on race. He speared John C. Bennett's inadequate earlier slighting of the race

---

3. Niebuhr, *Pious and Secular America*, 98.
4. Niebuhr, *Structure of Nations*, 213–16.
5. Edwards, "Niebuhr, Realism, and Civil Rights," 12–15.

issue, but Bennett was the president who integrated Union's faculty, including the Niebuhr-approved appointment of James Cone.[6] Incidentally, James Cone was enthusiastic about Edwards's essays while I was more critical in our discussion of this on 120th Street. I accept much of Edwards's criticism of realism and particularly his critique of Paul Ramsey. Henry Clark took Edwards more seriously than I did, but then Henry in his valuable book gave no evidence of reading the later more militant Niebuhr of the 1960s either.[7]

In addition to his ongoing critique of the moral failures of Protestant churches regarding social justice and race relations, Niebuhr posted his recommendations that Billy Graham include justice for the blacks among the fruits of his evangelism. He noted that the revivals of one hundred years earlier had strengthened the cause of abolitionism, and he hoped that the contemporary evangelists would regard racism as a sin that needed to be repented and ended. Billy noted the critique and began to reform his message. Graham and Niebuhr remained contestants in politics as Graham supported Republicans in general and anti-Catholicism in the 1960 election while Niebuhr remained left of central in his various political commitments. Norman Vincent Peale shared with me in Switzerland in 1961 how he resented Billy Graham abandoning him in their anti-Catholic polemic against John F. Kennedy. Union Theological Seminary supported the attack on the Graham-Peale group. My wife, Joan, worked for offices in the National Council of Churches building that attacked the anti-Catholic criticism of Kennedy. Peale was distressed that his son, John, was attending Union along with me. The four of us, John and his wife and I and my wife, traveling in Europe together joined Dr. Peale and his wife in Interlaken, Switzerland, for hikes in the mountains and meals. Dr. Peale was appeased some when he discovered how much John and I had learned about Scripture our first year at Union in a remedial Bible course. The young seminarians and spouses favored Kennedy while the older Peales maintained their critiques of the

---

6. Edwards, "Racism and Christian Ethics," 15–24.

7. Clark, *Serenity, Courage and Wisdom*, 157–58, 163–64.

10. Jews and Christians

Democrats. The Niebuhr critique of Graham continued even into the 1969 Niebuhr criticism of Graham in the Nixon White House chapel. Graham, between the two polemics, recognized Niebuhr's advice and adjusted his work a little. Before he finished this polemic about racism to Graham, Niebuhr quoted a Jewish friend who hoped Graham could include a word about Christian witness against racism because Jews and secularists could agree.[8]

By the end of the decade the inevitability of the hierarchical society of the United States was accepted by Niebuhr as the reality. We had not achieved a democracy, but a plutocracy. He told the story of American political thought as retaining some of its sentimentality of the dreamer thinking that liberty or equality could be achieved. Still the expansion of the US across the continent and the abundance of its natural resources had permitted movements toward equality and liberty. As the poor achieved unionization and suffrage and their power increased they could realize gains in dignity. We had failed miserably regarding the black race, but in 1957 Niebuhr could admit some optimism as they gained power by pressuring the Supreme Court for equality. The ideal of equality was pushed by the court in terms of justice upon the sordid reality of American race relations. In recognizing this he affirmed some of the idealism of *Does Civilization Need Religion?* The realism of *Moral Man and Immoral Society*, noting that the struggle for social justice required illusion as well as realism, was also apparent.[9] Further gains for black people toward justice required power and suffrage. Even as he sometimes criticized Martin Luther King Jr.'s illusions, he admired his realism. Niebuhr's lack of illusion did not mean he thought it should not be part of the mix of struggles for justice. Of note is the recognition that Niebuhr's thought usually referred to the experiences of the English and French Revolutions as well as the American. He could agree with Edmund Burke that the French lost their way in pursuit of unqualified egalitarianism. The egalitarian dreams of some of Cromwell's army could not be realized. Niebuhr celebrated the debates in the revolutionary army

8. Niebuhr, "Proposal to Billy Graham," 154–60.
9. Niebuhr, "Liberty and Equality," 185–98.

and affirmed the revolutionary Calvinism of some of the Puritans. Cromwell's tyranny led to the restoration of the monarchy, but now it was qualified by parliament. Without the monarchs, America settled into its plutocracy qualified by opportunity and the ideals of equality and liberty. Niebuhr fought as hard as any white theologian, and James Cone said he was the best white theologian on race.[10] He was free of some of our activist illusions. While we could sing, "Deep in our hearts we do believe we shall overcome some day," I cannot imagine Niebuhr believed that day was a historical day.

---

10. James Cone's remark to Ronald Stone, 2016.

11. Civil Rights Act of 1957

THE SAME YEAR NIEBUHR published the philosophical piece on liberty and equality he got down into the political weeds praising the Civil Rights Act of 1957. Like in the making of sausage, it is helpful not to give too sharp a look at how policy is made. Niebuhr's essay, "The Civil Rights Bill," details the compromises and concessions made to the South to pass the first civil rights legislation since the Reconstruction days. He recognized Senator Richard Russell's role in not filibustering the bill. School integration was not pushed in the bill, while the improvements in black suffrage were helping to eliminate the sanctions against integration. He quoted Martin Luther King Jr.: "Give us the vote and we will do the rest."[1] He saw moral issues and politics colliding and presenting their necessary compromises. He could claim it as a victory for democracy while recognizing other interests were preserved. He praised Johnson's shrewd compromises, but he feared Republican leadership might cost the Democrats black votes in the North. He worried about the increased political clout of Vice President Nixon. In September he feared a long, cold winter for Democrats and worried about probable losses for them in the elections. The FDR coalition, which led the Democrats to dominance in the South, continued to decline.

Niebuhr's official action on race relations in the late 1920s were not matched by other white pastors in that decade. Few pastors or ethics pastors had their denunciations of the Ku Klux Klan and white supremacists reported on the front pages of urban

---

1. Niebuhr, "Civil Rights Bill," 9.

newspapers during contested elections. His chairmanship of the Mayor's Interracial Committee, and the breadth of the report, stands out as an act of statesmanship and courage. In the 1930s his work is distinguished by the founding of the Fellowship of Socialist Christians, the Highlander School in Tennessee, and the Delta Farm in Mississippi as well as the essays commented on in this book. The forties saw his work on race expand to efforts on behalf of the Japanese in California and the outstanding labors to save the Jews. He and Paul Tillich regarded their efforts on behalf of the allies against Nazis as a war of liberation. The late 1940s and fifties were years of deliberation over nuclear weapons, wars in Asia and the beginnings of the civil rights struggle. The leadership from Martin Luther King Jr. and others in the fifties produced their fruit in the 1960s. The following statements by Niebuhr in the 1960s were as full-throated support for justice for blacks as the more militant James Cone could hope for.

Following his 1952 stroke and other disabilities, his energy was deserting him in the 1960s. I walked with him on Riverside Drive because his health required that he be accompanied. The one time I drove him to Union Seminary for his final speech there I described helping him into the car as shoveling him into the seat. President John Bennett and I conspired to provoke him into that last speech because we wanted to counter the student apathy of the time. His humor, analysis, and critical historical approach led the seminary into direct actions against the war. He would greet my letter from the Washington jail with the complaint that he wished he could participate. Ursula wrote me that on one occasion of getting up from his desk after writing me he fell flat on his face.[2] Two essays in our book, *Reformed Faith and Politics*, reflect his hopes that we were progressing on the issues of race. He seemed less pessimistic or that he had forgotten his earlier work that without access to property there is no freedom. He wrote:

> "This American Dilemma" is on the way to being resolved and one of the instruments of its resolution has proved to be the insistence on equality as a criterion of

2. Ursula Niebuhr, quoted in Stone, *Reinhold Niebuhr in the 1960s*, 150.

11. Civil Rights Act of 1957

justice.... We have in other words done tolerably well in transmuting sentiments into relevant criteria of justice.[3]

During this decade of the beginnings of action in the Supreme Court and Congress, his writing on race were two chapters in *Pious and Secular America* and twenty-five shorter pieces containing essays and editorials on civil rights, states' rights, Supreme Court decisions, Christianity and racism, interracial marriages, and a few pieces against apartheid in South Africa.

---

3. Niebuhr, "Liberty and Equality," 197–98.

12. The New Frontier

THOUGH NIEBUHR SUPPORTED STEVENSON until John F. Kennedy won the nomination, he supported Kennedy's campaign against Richard Nixon and expected Kennedy to be more forceful than President Eisenhower in supporting justice for blacks. He worried about Kennedy's womanizing and ruthlessness. Arthur Schlesinger assured him there would be no scandals in the White House, and Niebuhr reassured Schlesinger about the need for Johnson in the South. He introduced Kennedy at the Liberal Party convention and embarrassed him by a joke not to worry about the Pope controlling him, because the Pope could not even control his archbishop, the crowd except for Kennedy laughed. But, by the time of his 1963 eulogy for the young president he lionized his record and cheered his attempts for justice for blacks. Niebuhr's own record for integration and power for the black population also rose to new heights during the 1960s. Also relevant to his sharper critique of the southern stance on integration was that he no longer could travel there because of his various infirmities. His institutions, the Delta Cooperative Farm and the Highlander School, were forced to close under racist pressure from the White Citizens Council, and he no longer needed to appeal for funds to support them. Union Seminary, from which he retired in 1960, allied both with Kennedy and Martin Luther King Jr. until their assassinations provided an atmosphere for student and faculty social action. By the end of the decade it had called three black faculty: Larry Jones, Eric Lincoln, and James Cone.

12. The New Frontier

Many of the new students at Union in 1960 were enthusiastic about the church as they credited the black churchmen for inspiring the civil rights movement. Some, like myself, had also been inspired by white students from the churches and seminaries taking on the issues of racial justice. The ethos of Union reflected commitments of social transformation in the direction of justice. Soon after arrival I was persuaded to join in picketing the Woolworth's five-and-dime on 125th Street, the main shopping center of Harlem, in solidarity with black students integrating Woolworth's dining counters in the South. My fieldwork at Riverside Church, under the leadership of a black pastor, Robert Polk, and later in a community center on 124th Street, was with black youth in Harlem. I had to learn quickly about black education and mores as I led them to design worship services, and I coached basketball and boxing. Still only some of the Union students joined the picketing on the March on Washington, and fewer were arrested at the sit-in at the South African Embassy to protest the feared execution of Nelson Mandela. There were no black faculty and only a few black students in my class. Probably no students were aware of Niebuhr's long history of working for racial justice, but they knew a couple of the new younger faculty had been arrested in the South for integrating airport facilities. We read Niebuhr and other faculty pleading for social justice in *Christianity and Crisis*. Though only a few students acted directly, the seminary ethos knew racism was sinful and that the churches and social institutions needed to change. Niebuhr's farewell speech to the seminary in 1960 still decried the white church's failure on the race relations issues. He did, however, in light of Martin Luther King Jr.'s work, praise the black church for its renewal on the issue. He called for the church to primarily engage two issues: the threats of nuclear war and the race relations crisis. The addition of political philosophy to those two provided the major agenda for the last decade of his life. The Niebuhrs moved from the seminary to 304 Riverside Drive in 1960, and a grant from the Rockefeller Foundation encouraged him to join the War and Peace Seminar at Columbia University and to give his seminar for one more year at the seminary. The next three years would see him teaching at Harvard, Princeton, and Barnard before returning to Union for the last years of his seminar.

Niebuhr's first article on race in 1960 dealt with the racism against the black population of South Africa, which was the closest thing to slavery on earth. He joined Alan Paton in finding little hope for change there. The government of South Africa seemed determined to pursue a course to inevitable disaster. The policies of the Dutch Reformed church were akin to those of the Nazis. In his writing in this last decade of his life he often referred to the racism of white supremacists as akin to Nazism. He praised the burgeoning movement to expel the Dutch church from the World Council of Churches while finding a little hope in the English-speaking churches of South Africa. "The 'German Christians' were both inhumane and heretical. The African white church is obscurantist and inhumane."[1]

His major essay on race in 1961 began and ended with the narrative of white women hissing like geese against the four black girls attempting to integrate the New Orleans school. The thrust of the article was that around the world the black peoples were rising against white arrogance from South Africa to Algeria. Even with China he thought white arrogance was more a source of resentment than communism. The world needed the skills of Europe without the white arrogance. Russia, in seeming less European, had advantages in this tide of color rising in the world. The West needed to provide skills and tools to the black world "without revealing the fact that the white man tends to be a Nazi with kid gloves, but still a kind of Nazi."[2] *Christianity and Crisis* produced a special issue on race, edited by Roger Shinn, analyzing the civil rights movement and introducing its readers to Eric Lincoln through a review of his book on black nationalism. Professor Lincoln would join the Union faculty and eventually I would enjoy the honor of working with him on a master of arts thesis from an outstanding student he mentored in sociology of religion. Niebuhr wrote in the next issue on "The Montgomery Savagery." He called for the severe

1. Niebuhr, "Church and the South African Tragedy," 54.
2. Niebuhr, "Rising Tide of Color," 16.

enforcement of the law: "The Whip of the law cannot change the heart. But thank God it can restrain the heartless until they change their mind and heart."[3] To my mind, Niebuhr's development on the race issue and willingness to use the full power of the government, when it could be persuaded to act, had been reached by this point in 1961.

The next year he commented on race prejudice seeming to be the most "recalcitrant aspect of the evil in man."[4] He approved of Edmund Wilson's suggestion that Mississippi and Alabama should have been allowed to secede except for the fact that their forced adherence to the Union prevented them from becoming as impossible as South Africa. The national community and confessed values were of some effect even in those states. Still it was only Eisenhower's reluctant use of force that allowed James Meredith to integrate the University of Mississippi. Force could accomplish that which local conscience opposed. Neither the North nor Christianity had any reason to gloat, as only the government with force could accomplish the moral task.[5]

King took his nonviolent movement to Birmingham in 1963 to negotiate an end to white supremacy in that particularly dangerously segregated city. It refused to bend. By April, King was in jail. He responded to the criticism from eight white Alabama clergy of his movement, his timing, his tactics, and his passion for change. His response, the "Letter from Birmingham Jail," became a classic of the civil rights movement, and a primary document of US history. It was soon reprinted in Niebuhr's journal *Christianity and Crisis*. King's mastery of Niebuhr's work and the use of nonviolent tactics in a Gandhian manner to win justice over massive violence was explained in his "Letter." The evil of racist institutional loyalties was explained in a paraphrase of Niebuhr's words from *Moral Man and Immoral Society*. King had studied Niebuhr in Crozer Seminary, and he knew his thought well enough to use it without his textbooks.

3. Niebuhr, "Montgomery Savagery," 103.
4. Niebuhr, "Intractability of Race Prejudice," 181.
5. Niebuhr, "Intractability of Race Prejudice," 181.

Niebuhr's articles against racism sometimes repeated the same arguments. His lecture in the religion department at Barnard in 1963 leveled fresh criticism at the most segregated hour of the week as the Protestant church services on Sunday at 11 AM. Harold Stahmer, professor at Barnard, included the lecture in his collection of essays on religion in America.[6] Though Barnard on 122nd Street was only a few blocks from Harlem, Niebuhr's lecture was the only one on race. His regular essay for *The Christian Century* called the churches to take seriously the dangers of nuclear weapons and race relations, but this year Niebuhr emphasized race more than the nuclear danger. Most of us in the halls at Union did not notice the shift. Though he had used Gunnar Myrdal's term "dilemma" before, he now spurned it and referred to the race crisis as a tragedy.[7]

He recorded his changed view of the black church. "The Negro church in the person of Dr. Martin Luther King has validated itself in the life of the Negroes and of the nation."[8] He thought the black revolution was going to reach its goals and that the morals of the nation were expressing their relevance though the expected success of the civil rights legislation. White supremacy was facing its defeat even though its murderous resistance was increasing. He repeated his criticism of the failure of the white church, but he celebrated the effectiveness of other cultural institutions and the hopefulness that the government was now decisively on the side of overcoming racism.

6. Niebuhr, "Religious Situation," 150.
7. Niebuhr, "Crisis in Protestantism," 1499.
8. Niebuhr, "Mounting Racial Crisis," 121.

13. Birmingham Bombing

Two months after Niebuhr's hopeful essay, the children were bombed in their Sunday school in Birmingham. Martin Luther King Jr. eulogized them in the paraphrased words of Horatio: "Goodnight sweet princesses may the flight of angels take thee to eternal rest."[1] In New York City Niebuhr and James Baldwin were brought together to discuss the murderous act, which King had described "as one of the most heinous crimes ever perpetuated against humanity."[2]

The 16th Street Baptist Church in Birmingham was bombed on September 15, 1963, killing four children—Denise McNair, Addie May Collins, Carole Robertson, and Cynthia Wesley—on their way to Sunday School. The Protestant Council of New York immediately called James Baldwin and Reinhold Niebuhr to discuss the bombing on the radio, moderated by a former student of Niebuhr's, Thomas Kilgore, then pastor of Friendship Baptist Church and director of the Southern Leadership Conference in New York City. Their unpublished dialogue is in the Niebuhr Papers of the Library of Congress. James Cone and I frequently discussed this dialogue and we both have written on it before.[3]

Kilgore began the discussion with the broken symbol of Christ's face from the wreckage. Baldwin understood it as a symbol of the white church's failure to love across the color line.

1. King, "Eulogy," 223.

2. King, "Eulogy," 221.

3. Niebuhr, "Meaning of the Tragedy"; Stone, *Politics and Faith*, 431–33; Cone, *Cross and the Lynching Tree*, 53–57.

Niebuhr took it as a symbol of the white church's failure to find a way to pursue racial justice. They agreed on the failure of the white church to live up to its creed. Niebuhr did not expect the races to love each other, but he pleaded for justice.

Niebuhr claimed to have read all of Baldwin's works. He knew that Baldwin had been a preacher in his youth. They both had preacher fathers. Baldwin's father had rejected the young James, and James had given up on Christ. Niebuhr kept the Christ of his youth in his heart, and his father had encouraged him in his ministry. Baldwin had dined with Elijah Muhammad and affirmed with him that the white man was a devil. The despair of blacks had been captured in his "The Fire Next Time" as movingly as by any writer of the time. The system that the whites ruled may not have intended the bombing, but it certainly ground the hope out of black children. Niebuhr's own recognition of the Nazi-like quality of the racist system of the United States may have been as strong a condemnation as Baldwin or Cone's use of the symbol of the devil. But, Niebuhr admitted, he could not identify with black suffering.

Unless the racially enlightened whites could join the self-conscious blacks and end the racial oppression, Baldwin knew the country was doomed. If the anti-racist minorities could not join together to change the country and the world all was lost. "God gave Noah the rainbow sign. No more water, the fire next time."[4] Niebuhr's pragmatism was less apocalyptic. Niebuhr hoped for change through education, the courts, politics, boycotts, and demonstrations. Baldwin, feeling the suffering more, was the more powerful in the conversation. The aging, disabled Niebuhr may have needed a few more months to reach Baldwin's level of anger, but by then the cities would be burning. Baldwin would have moved to self-imposed exile, and Malcolm X would have been assassinated by the henchmen of Elijah Muhammad. Niebuhr commented on the renewal of the black church by Martin Luther King Jr. as one of the great present Americans. Baldwin agreed with Niebuhr's praise of the black church and regarded them as the only active Christians in America. He said:

4. Baldwin, "Fire Next Time," 105–6.

13. Birmingham Bombing

> It is ironical, I am trying to say. That the people who were slaves here, the most beaten and despised people here, and for so long would at this moment, and I mean this absolutely are the only hope in this country. It doesn't have any other.

In the dialogue Baldwin used prophetic language and Niebuhr sometimes used revolutionary language, but they both believed in coalition politics to overcome the oppression and advance integration. Baldwin moved on to Niebuhr's ground speaking about the irresponsibility of the white majority. He did not blame all whites in Birmingham for bombing the girls, but he regarded the whites who controlled Birmingham as irresponsible. He regarded the silence of whites as criminally irresponsible. Baldwin hoped Washington, DC could enforce the integration of the neighborhoods so the schools would follow.

The moderator asked Niebuhr about the church, as you would expect an agent of the Protestant Council to do. Niebuhr took the bait to criticize the individualism of the Protestant church as you would expect of any follower of the social gospel. Niebuhr again praised the leadership of King and his sparking of the black church. I do not think Niebuhr ever mentioned the resistance in the black church to King's movement. Love was the motive for struggling in the conflict, but the tools of justice were the way forward. The moderator asked Baldwin about boycotting Christmas shopping. Both Baldwin and Niebuhr would approve, but neither expected it to be effective. The concept of arming black people was more attractive to Baldwin than Niebuhr who believed more deeply in King's nonviolent strategy for the minority. The two sparred a little about tactics, but basically they agreed on the major issues. Cone and I both believed that Baldwin showed more passion and fire, and I, knowing of Niebuhr's aging pains and his own diffidence as a white man, regarded the greater passion of both the younger Cone and Baldwin as inevitable. In conclusion, the moderator announced a couple of community meetings to continue the reflection and thanked both speakers.

Even the "Letter from Birmingham Jail" signaled how desperate the struggle for justice was becoming. The white backlash utilized murder and intimidation, and the black commitment to nonviolent mass action was weakening. In 1964, Niebuhr warned against the coming violent summer season and beyond. He understood it would take decades to achieve a "genuine multiracial community."[5] His use of tribalism to describe the racist commitments of different ethnic groups pointed toward his development, in his later book, that black people were the hope. He wanted readers to understand that though the power of the law was used to desegregate society, white resistance still prevented the integration of schools or neighborhoods. The black person was kept inferior by the denial of his full rights to life and dignity. *De facto* segregation in both the South and the North was still the rule. The states of the old Confederacy and the white backlash in the North preserved the rule of white supremacy. There was more progress than in South Africa, where apartheid was legal, but the whites in the US were "unheeding" of the suffering of the blacks. The tools of the integrationists were weak, as suffrage without jobs was inadequate to overcome the blinding poverty of the racial minority. Niebuhr kept advocating for the consumer boycott, but he knew it was not as strong as the laborers had found in the ability to organize the working class and demand the deserved change. The stubbornness of racial prejudice was stronger than the hatred of race prejudice, so "the struggle for racial justice is a long and tough one."[6]

---

5. Niebuhr, "Man, the Unregenerate Tribalist," 133.
6. Niebuhr, "Man, the Unregenerate Tribalist," 134.

14. *Mississippi Black Paper*

RANDOM HOUSE ASKED NIEBUHR to provide the foreword to *Mississippi Black Paper*, which collected the documents testifying to the injustice of the state by the Council of Federated Organizations. In that state the supposed tools of justice served injustice to preserve white supremacy. It required federal power to return the state to the American principles confessed by the country. Mississippi was corrupting its courts and police so badly that murder in defense of racism could not be prosecuted. Local jury trials freed murderers of civil rights workers and could not convict the killers of Medgar Evers. The documents proved, he said, that when social discipline broke down as in South Africa, Germany, and some Southern states, cruelty flourished. They also showed the need for the proposed civil rights law. "Justice in Mississippi is corrupted to such a degree that without aid from outside it is doomed."[1]

Finally in 1965, Niebuhr could celebrate the fact that the nation's major religions were united in working to overcome the oppression of black people. The murder of James Reeb inspired nationwide grief and put the white oligarchy on notice that its racist power was declining. The march on the capitol of Alabama was protected by President Johnson federalizing the National Guard of the state. Still the federal government lacked the power to prosecute the murderers of blacks and their white allies. A century was too long to wait for the rights supposedly won in the Civil War, and the black frustration was a combination of their misery and

---

1. Niebuhr, "Foreword," in *Mississippi Black Paper*, n.p.

increased hopes.[2] He was hopeful for the coming civil rights bill and some of his students were active both in Alabama and Washington, DC. The editor of his journal, Wayne Cowan, joined the march from Selma to Montgomery.

Ursula and Reinhold were supportive of my going to Oxford to continue my study of political philosophy, and Herbert Deane, a Columbia professor of political philosophy, regarded John Plamenatz of Nufield College as the best in the world. I loved Oxford, my son Randall was born there, and Joan was busy helping John Macquarrie prepare his book on philosophy of religion. The boxing team wanted me as captain for the next year, and I looked forward to the exams for a graduate degree in the following year. Life there was very good. A letter from Dean Roger Shinn of Union invited me to return to assist him and Reinhold Niebuhr for 1966–67. We returned to Union and while writing my dissertation I assisted Professors Shinn, Bennett, and Niebuhr. So I worked for Niebuhr's seminar in his home from 1966–68 until his final retirement to Stockbridge. Walking with him each Friday afternoon was the best education I received, and it followed his vision of the best education from Johns Hopkins, with a teacher and a student sitting on a log. We lacked the log, but we walked among the trees of Riverside Drive for those two years. Every year the seminar included one or two sessions on race, and it usually covered anti-Semitism and American racism. The seminar had been one of his regular courses. He usually taught a large two-semester ethics course, which contained the ethics of world religions in the first semester and Christian ethics in the second semester. Following his year sabbatical at the Institute of Advanced Study at Princeton with George Kennan he added a new course on the moral issues in international relations, which included the content of his *The Structure of Nations and Empires*. He regularly taught a course on "Christianity and Communism" with other colleagues. I participated in the seminar in 1964 as a doctoral student at Columbia. I wrote a paper on the political philosophy of Hans Morgenthau. He asked me to stop by his apartment after he read the paper. I

---

2. Niebuhr, "Civil Rights Climax in Alabama," 1.

14. MISSISSIPPI BLACK PAPER

was amazed he knew exactly which pages of my paper he wanted to discuss, and my visit became an appreciative tutorial on Morgenthau's thought. It became the basis for our later work together. By 1966, the racial conflicts were becoming more evident, and he spent more time on the black-white conflicts and his work on anti-Semitism was focused more at Jewish Theological Seminary, which published his last major paper. Out of his appreciation of Niebuhr, President Finklestein of Jewish Theological Seminary invited me and my wife to his Seder meal.

15. The Seminar

THE FOLLOWING DISCUSSION OF his seminar is from his notes for the 1966 seminar. He would type out a rough outline of the course for his lecture and the second half of the course was largely discussion of student research papers, which were often their senior thesis papers as the course was designed for seniors and graduate students who were already familiar with Christian social ethics. The discussion of race relations was preceded in the seminar by his lectures on biblical and philosophical development of ethical themes leading to reflection on equality, freedom, and order as constitutive of social justice. By the time he was giving the course he had published *Man's Nature and His Communities* and he emphasized the tribal nature of racism. He taught that all nations depend upon bonds of race and language to hold themselves together. Language was easier than race to hold in common and both England and America had used English as a bond. As the US attempted a "melting pot," the public schools brought the immigrants together on the basis of the common language. The discussion here reflected his own experience as a German-speaking youth who developed his English into a powerful tool.

Still he taught that tribalism was the most vicious source of "man's inhumanity to man." Tribalism often thwarted the development of an integral human community. Often tribalism was distinguished by language. The European nations overcame the common language of Latin and the remnants of empire to assert their independence. Religion, racial origins, or culture or class could also serve to strengthen tribalism. He briefly spoke of the

15. The Seminar

tribalism of Cyprus, Nigeria, and the Congo. The tyrannies of tribalism expressed in Nazi Germany, South Africa, and Mississippi, could become more damaging than open conflict in Niebuhr's estimation. The racial dimension took on characteristics of class discrimination in the caste system of India, discrimination in Latin America, and the brutality of the American system. Tribalism contradicted the universal quality of humanity asserted in stoicism, Christianity, and modern anthropology. Niebuhr quoted Cicero[1] in his book more strongly than other authorities to recognize the common humanity of all grounded in reason. Early Christianity inherited much of its universalism from stoicism and joined it to its Hebrew prophetic heritage. The laws focusing on human rights were reducing the tribalism in the modern world. But in the US the tribalism continued in a brutal fashion in racial discrimination. Both in his own presentation and in the book[2] he recommended for the course, the struggle for overcoming tribalism or racism was a long, slow process. Niebuhr thought it might take one hundred years. Fifty years after the seminar, his estimate seems appropriate. Though, he feared that such a recognition would be criticized as an exhortation to slow down. I think it was the realism of Griswold and Niebuhr that led them both to the observation that the evil was resistant to elimination. The victory in India by lower classes is now encouraging more drastic forms of discrimination against Muslims.

The denial of education to black people left them bereft of skills needed for modern employment. The color difference and their low-class opportunities combined to make their oppression hard to overcome. The caste systems of India and the US were both based in color, conquest, and vocation, which reinforced discrimination in other areas.

There were contradictions in the American history of racism. The Declaration of Independence both affirmed human equality and deplored slaves joining the British for an opportunity for freedom. The Constitution was a compromise to bind the Southern

1. Niebuhr, *Man's Nature*, 91–92.
2. Griswold, *Law and Lawyers*, chapter 5.

colonies to the Northern colonies. It held until the Civil War, which no one wanted to repeat. The Civil War gains and the amendments to the Constitution were soon surrendered for short-term political gain. Niebuhr had often repeated that there was little justice for those without property. The South was appeased, and the Supreme Court decisions attempting to supply equality without integration failed. A century after the Civil War the workers of black complexion were still serfs in the South and discriminated against in the North. Griswold's book assigned for the seminar provided the data proving the sadness of the American settlement, which Niebuhr's Mayor's Report on Race in Detroit had indicated forty years earlier.

Niebuhr reflected on his interpretations of King's bus boycott in Montgomery, students striving for integration, and the Supreme Court decisions moving the agenda of racial progress forward. He celebrated black victories in politics. Still, without property, union organization, or enough modern technological skills, progress was slow.

He spoke of a black revolution and understood the blacks to be the real proletariat in the American system. They were living in a middle class paradise while being prevented from participating. The blacks had little power to use. The struggle resembled to Niebuhr the labor movement's fight toward the New Deal. He regarded the cries of "black power" as illusory. He saw hope in black suffrage and the civil rights laws of the 1960s. He noted the desperation of the black unemployed. He tried to place the black revolution in terms of a new class struggle. I knew from our discussions later that he was looking for new words to enliven the struggle, and to win allies in the white population. He did not yet have a strong estimate of the black church's participation. Probably more gains could be won through black politics than he saw at the time. He knew of Nixon's playing of the race card and the pushing of the Democratic party to the sideline in the South.

The black and white cooperation in the Urban League and NAACP had preceded the revolution, and the road of politics seemed to be opening up, but it was precarious. He also spoke of white reactions, noting help from liberal writers in politics and

15. The Seminar

law. He praised Catholic leaders for gains in integrating parochial schools, and in the Bishop's public stands. Protestants in the South continued in their irrelevance or acquiescence to racial injustice, and most of the white churches in the North did not practice integration. Whites were still dodging school and housing integration in the North. He saw signs of hope in the appointment of the presidential national advisory commission on national civil disorders. A couple of years later he would write on this commission's work for a magazine I was editing. He was also beginning his critique of the Vietnam War with which he agreed with Martin Luther King Jr. King would join the organization founded at Union with Niebuhr's participation: Clergy and Laity Concerned about Vietnam. The course in which Niebuhr assigned books by black authors was "Ethical Viewpoints in Modern Literature," which he had inherited from his coteaching of the class with Harry Ward. There he assigned James Weldon Johnson, Langston Hughes, and Countee Cullen. Dietrich Bonhoeffer took the course and read these authors, according to James Cone.[3] However, Cone praises Bonhoeffer for his passion for involving himself with blacks while in America, while criticizing Niebuhr for his lack of interest in black culture. As Union first-year students, we took a tour of relevant social justice actors in New York. A. Philip Randolph spoke movingly about his association with Reinhold Niebuhr. Even at much later meetings of the American Academy of Religion a black intellectual spoke enthusiastically about Niebuhr's counseling of black ministers of Harlem while he criticized an important white intellectual for not mentioning these meetings in his book on liberation.

Niebuhr's most interesting contribution to racial justice in 1967 was his defense of Martin Luther King Jr. He wrote the foreword to the four speeches against the Vietnam War sponsored by Clergy and Laymen Concerned about Vietnam.[4] He chose not to comment on speeches by his friends John C. Bennett and Abraham Heschel, but focused on King's speech to counter the criticism of

---

3. Cone, *Cross and the Lynching Tree*, 42.
4. Niebuhr, "Foreword," in *Dr. Martin Luther King Jr.*, 3.

King for engaging on Vietnam. He hoped for the churches to adopt a common cause against the prosecution of the war, and he noted the opposition within many of the universities. He noted that some civil rights leaders feared King's position against the war would weaken the civil rights struggle. However, King, as one of the great religious leaders, had a right to speak on humanitarian issues. He also defended King's program of nonviolent resistance and it was not one of absolute pacifism. His nonviolent resistance is a great contribution to American moral life. The criticism of King weakened some people's affection for the race relations struggle, and it broke the support of him by the Johnson administration. It probably hastened his death. On the other hand, I think Niebuhr's endorsement helped weaken support for the war by some and discouraged some others from criticism of King's choice.

16. After King's Murder

NIEBUHR'S CRITIQUE OF RACISM came to fulfillment in 1968. "A Question of Priorities"[1] joined his critique of U. S. Policy in Vietnam to his concern for racial justice. He weighed the debt we owed to the racial minority to the vase expenditures in treasure and the lives of young Americans in Asia. To him it was obvious that racial justice here was the priority. The necessity of uniting the states outweighed the illusions of equality in our founding documents. Neither the equality of Jefferson nor Lincoln was desired in the slave states. They spouted romantic illusions. The forefathers were not so much hypocrites, they just desired the union of an empire and the profits from slavery. The Civil War freed the slave from bondage, but condemned him to poverty. The following amendments expressed hopes for citizenship, but they were overcome by violence. Following years revealed the truth that laws cannot be enforced without community support. Conscience without power cannot right substantial wrongs. Niebuhr often used the word dismal to describe America society.

But what about the gains of the civil rights movement and the new legislation? Its victories have placed some black people in places of public office and power. But the unemployment and poverty remain. Schools are still segregated, as is housing. The explosions of violence in the cities are not part of the black revolution, they only express frustration and desperation. Referring to Karl Marx, Niebuhr saw black people as the proletariat without

---

1. Niebuhr, "Question of Priorities," 9–11.

power to change social fundamentals. The boycott had produced some gains, as did nonviolent tactics, but Niebuhr could not see black people having any effective tool like the union strikes. He believed the Johnson administration was serious in its war against poverty. However the Vietnam War inclined Congress to reject funds for its pursuit and chose to throw away America's strength in its silly fighting for "democracy" in a former French colony, and to save US pride in Vietnam. The original policy for Vietnam was mistaken, and the cost of covering it up was too high. The failure of Roman Catholic Mandarins governing Buddhist peasants was inevitable. The first religious protests at Union Theological Seminary against the Kennedy war policy were inspired by suicidal protests of Buddhist priests against the Nhu family and Madam Nhu's high-handed dismissal of their concerns. Niebuhr believed that many people thought the black minority needed justice now and they were demanding the cessation of the US killing in Vietnam. He saw the new priorities being built on a moral judgment that had no relationship to the older isolationism.

Niebuhr's second major essay on race, "The Negro Minority and Its Fate in a Self-Righteous Nation," repeated the themes of his essay on priorities and discussed more thoroughly the churches' roles. He reviewed again the canyon between the nation's ideals and its practice. He found black poverty to be due to unemployment from inadequate education and white prejudice. The American illusions of righteousness seen in both Jefferson and Lincoln thwarted efforts to expose the reality of oppression. The black minority had little power to change the reality and consequently the burden of moral responsibility rested with the national government. The overcoming of the denial of the vote was the central road block on progress toward justice. He noted how the energy of the civil rights movement drew upon both economic desperation and hope.

He thought the National Advisory Commission's report on black frustration and anger was correct and that only by creating more economic justice could the violence be avoided. The commission had not been surprised by the riots of 1967–68, and it

16. After King's Murder

understood correctly how black anger was set against both the welfare system and the economic system. The relatively wealthy white culture was complacent regarding the oppression of black people, as its idealism and individualism blinded it to the injustice of a divided country.

The churches were guilty of sins of commission and omission. They were segregated and denied worship to blacks and they failed their prophetic function of calling attention to the nation's sins. He quoted Benjamin Mays, "The Protestant church hour, eleven o'clock Sunday morning is the most segregated hour of the week."[2]

His recommendations included integrating local churches and he celebrated that such were growing, but the power of black congregations in correcting injustices meant they needed preservation as a power base for change. The interracial meetings at regional, local, and national conferences needed to be developed. He mentioned the YMCA and YWCA interracial conferences, which had met for some time. The church was and ought to be involved in reforming the welfare system. He commented favorably on the "Negative Income Tax." He supported more strongly a system of scholarships for those below an established poverty line. He recommended the commission's recommendations become agenda items for the returning congressional session. Without serious adjustments the rioting would continue. The country, he argued, had an agenda and the resources to equip its black minority if it had the will. He knew commission reports were limited in power, and this volume uses the two—his report of 1926 and the Advisory Commission's report in 1968—as bookends for this study. The final paragraphs of the essay reflect the conclusions and the style of the essay.

> The report of the Commission is full of suggested programs to alleviate the injustices this complacent nation has enforced upon the Negro minority. The Commission's priorities deserve to be the order of business for the returning Congress and the newly elected government. The alternative to taking the Commission seriously is

2. Niebuhr, "Negro Minority," 61.

continued rioting. The rioting and ambushes of 1968 are even more ominous than those of 1967. The Commission has shown the way to correct the most grievous injustices, if the nation can muster the moral will realistically to meet the crisis.

All these old and new provisions should not be negated because of expense. It is the high priority of an affluent society to lift the poor Negro minority from the vicious circle [of] technical ignorance, even illiteracy, sickness, and crime. It is certainly a higher priority than our military involvement in the civil war of an obscure nation. This futile war is costing us billions, while the problem of the helpless Negro minority, costing half as much, has not been met. After almost two centuries of broken promises and pledges our debt to our Negro minority is immense and obvious, and its burden lies heavy upon our conscience.[3]

After 1968, less than three years of his life remained, but there were three more issues on race to mention. "The King's Chapel and the King's Court"[4] was a critique of President Nixon's creation of a White House chapel to ensure religious support for his administration. The preachers tended to fawn over Nixon's policies. Niebuhr roared his disgust at Nixon's use of religion and found it particularly egregious regarding the continuation of the war in Vietnam. In this nearly last article he criticized Billy Graham's teaching on race, which seemed to assume individualism without regard to social structures. He referred back to Amos, his major prophet, and to Martin Luther King Jr.'s use of him in the March on Washington.

> I hate, I despise your feasts, and I take no delight in your solemn assemblies. . . . Take away from me the noise of your songs; to the melody of your harps I will not listen. But let justice role down like waters, and righteousness like an ever flowing stream. (Amos 5:21, 23–24.)

---

3. Niebuhr, "Negro Minority," 63–64.
4. Niebuhr, "King's Chapel," 211–12.

16. After King's Murder

Niebuhr said it was unfortunate that King was killed before he could be invited to the White House, but then he wondered if he could have been invited had he lived. Niebuhr had learned in seminary to relate Amos to present social issues. He musingly related J. Edgar Hoover to the court chaplain who refused Amos permission to preach in Samaria. It is unclear if Niebuhr knew that the Nixon administration was again examining the files Hoover had collected on him. But he knew of the FBI's spying on King and their attacks on him. Niebuhr reflected on establishment religion favoring conservatism, but he wondered if the critical voices of religion advocating criticism and justice could have been heard in the White House. He urged those asked to preach in the White House to reflect on Amos for they risked endorsing the regime. The essay received piles of critique, including my newspaper in Pittsburgh. When I wrote defending Niebuhr, I received my first anonymous death threat. The application of prophetic religion to politics continues to be dangerous. After this essay my friend, James Cone, announced "Niebuhr sounded surprisingly like Malcolm X."[5] Cone remained proud that Niebuhr had recommended him as a professor at Union, even as he criticized him.

In early 1970, Niebuhr sent me his new essay, "The Student Strike Against the War and Our National Self Interest." I wrote him after reviewing it saying I thought he misunderstood the students, and had listened too long to professors from Columbia who were disenchanted by the student revolt and occupation in 1968. He had been particularly disappointed in the occupation of Union in support of board members paying reparations for black projects. Whereas he had supported nonviolent campaigns heartily, he scolded Students for a Democratic Society and the Black Panthers for their attempts at revolution. I suggested he not publish it and he decided not to publish, but used some of his material in a shorter essay in the *New Leader*.[6] In the reduced article he compared the current revolutionary struggle to the labor struggles of the 1930s.

---

5. Cone, *Cross and the Lynching Tree*, 57.
6. Niebuhr, "Indicting Two Generations," 13–14.

He found the struggle in 1970 to be radically different from the 1930s actions.

The student revolt presently lacked strong support from labor, which had begun to balance industrial tycoons' power following the New Deal. A welfare state was being developed, and labor basically gave up on violent class struggle. The Vietnam War remained the main source of anger among the students. The struggle for equal justice for blacks remained a source of strife. Unemployment, inadequate housing, and segregated education drove the Black Panther Party to bitterness. The culture had failed in developing an ethical society and while demands for reforming education were among the students' complaints, their real issue was distrust of the establishment.

> The Black Panthers and SDS . . . are Stalinist or Maoist in that they engage in violence of every kind, from the occupation of college buildings to arson against ROTC headquarters to battles with policemen. Rock throwing and lead-pipe fusillades seem to be their standard revolutionary response.[7]

The rage against the society was also partially prompted by the failure of clean drinking water and air pollution as well as racial injustice not being addressed by the leaders of society. Some of the leaders would reply to criticism that violence was a rational act in a failed society. To Niebuhr the students were reacting to mistakes of their elders and therefore he called for an indictment of both generations. "The violence resulting from the destruction of the young over American society's sterility, however, will certainly complicate rather than cure, the problem which prompted it."[8]

In the longer unpublished piece he had celebrated black leaders elected to public office, and had recommended that students campaigning to elect senators in favor of peace in Vietnam would accomplish more than rioting and trashing campuses. In summary, his late-term policies focused on politics for the development

---

7. Niebuhr, "Indicting Two Generations," 14.
8. Niebuhr, "Indicting Two Generations," 14.

16. After King's Murder

of the welfare state and for limiting the imperial reach through warfare of the American superpower.[9]

He had one more contribution toward racial justice. In 1970 with the assistance of Ursula Niebuhr he wrote to the American Revolution Bicentennial Commission urging a discussion of the history of development of the nation, and recognizing three problems that needed addressing. He urged the commission to focus on the role of a superpower in avoiding nuclear war. He urged policies of ecological responsibility, particularly with reference to air and water. His first priority was: "The elimination of the last remnants of injustice, which slavery had introduced into our democratic society, and which since the Supreme Court decision of 1954 became ever and ever more urgent."[10]

Niebuhr's critique of white supremacy deepened in the 1960s, but no white theologian wrote against white hatred as consistently or as long as Niebuhr. His realism and pragmatism gave his contribution a less radical critique than some, but Cone's comment that he sounded like Malcolm X notes the radical anger of some of his pages. He was a professor of social ethics, which is a wider field than race relations, and his attention was often taken up by the persecution of Jews. He failed to take major note in his writing of the discrimination, wars against, and slavery of Native Americans.

His overall program provides maximum tactics and strategies for whites fighting against racism: Use anthropology and sociology when they are helpful against racism; follow study commission suggestions to overcome racism when they are useful; work to integrate housing and schools using the force of government when applicable; support demonstrations for social equality for the oppressed; raise and give funds for the development of social institutions against racism; support politics and the use of government force to prevent discrimination; preach and teach about racism; integrate faculties; oppose racism in the police force; note black achievements; recognize progress in race relations when possible;

---

9. Niebuhr, "The Student Strike Against War and Our National Self-discovery" (unpublished, copy in author's possession).

10. Niebuhr, "Memorandum on Bicentennial."

recognize the superiority of nonviolent tactics when they succeed (Gandhi and King); support voting legislation and lobby legislators; provide the poor with economic support and win the right to work for those discriminated against; lobby to legislate against lynching (See: FBI report and *The Daily Worker*); obtain church support for institutional development where needed, as in Delta Farm and Highlander School; stay loyal to church and improve its record in race relations; pursue politics to end the separation that breeds racism; make combating racism a personal priority; and utilize black authors in teaching; avoid self-righteousness in the struggle.

I think all of these tactics and strategies are represented in Niebuhr's life and writing, and they are discussed in this volume. The program to overcome American racism must be a broad one to be fought with idealism and realism.

Most Americans will not undertake as complete a program against racism as Niebuhr accomplished. I wish he had been more subtle in discussing the Founding Fathers, of whom he said they were not immoral just because they were slave holders. He could have said the founders of the nation participate in the universal human sin and that they carried more guilt than many because they participated in destroying the Native population and administering a slaveholding nation. Just as warriors in the revolution and in the administration of power they accrued more guilt than the average citizen.

Too often he opined on the cultural backwardness of black people, which was due to the historical suffering under slavery and white supremacy. James Baldwin spoke and wrote about the dangerous tendency to internalize white supremacy in blacks. It now seems quaint that he thought he needed to write so often how black people won recognition of equality.

Some black authors think he made too much out of gains by blacks during his own long lifetime. He wrote a little about the welfare system favoring one-parent families, but he could have detailed more about instruments of black oppression. The commissions he wrote about—The Mayor's Commission in Detroit

16. After King's Murder

(1926) and the National Advisory Committee—in the 1968 essay in his denominational magazine provided a lot of details noted above. A lot of his writing on race was more abstract than detailed. Neither he nor I have fulfilled identifying with the black race. A black faculty member that I worked to bring to the seminary preached that earlier he had been excluded from white churches. That is beyond my experience, and I have always been welcomed heartily to black churches. Blacks experience contains hurts that I want to overcome, but I cannot identify with their experience. Neither Niebuhr nor myself could pass the antiracism test or screen of Ibram X. Kendi.[11] Niebuhr fulfilled the criteria of antiracism better than I have and in all probability better than other white journalist-theologians. Tracy West's recent essay notes how much effort he brought to the fight against racism,[12] but if I understand her, she notes that his empathy could have been greater, and he would have agreed.

A note is made that ever since the 1926 mayor's report, the friendship and respect for the Jewish lawyer on the task force, Fred Butzel, translated into respect for the Jewish commitment to social justice. He became an important friend of the Jewish people as well as blacks. His writing and political work on their behalf is well-known. He also won the praise and support of American Japanese people for his criticism of their confinement on the West Coast in World War II. James Cone and I have noted his lack of reflection on the subjugation of the Native American in his reflections on American history. The 1619 project was an advance in the scholarship on race since his death.[13] His writing on tribalism and caste preceded the important book on caste by a few decades.[14] Ursula Niebuhr treasured the essay published posthumously by the Jewish Theological Seminary.[15] In places her editing is noticeable, and it rounds out his affection for his Jewish friends. It is mostly a

---

11. Paul, "Antiracism," A22.
12. West, "Racial Justice," 501–22.
13. Hannah-Jones, "1619 Project."
14. Wilkerson, *Caste*.
15. Niebuhr, "Mission and Opportunity."

review of interreligious history with some new theological analysis reminiscent of his *Nature and Destiny of Man,* but with more of a comparison of similar themes in Judaism. The essay deals more with the controversial anti-Jewish polemics in the Gospel of John than he had in previous writing. Throughout the work, the relativities of religious faiths introduced by historical situations and controversies is noted. Its concluding paragraphs deal with the development of Roman Catholic-Protestant dialogue with an emphasis upon the nonnegotiable issues. His appreciation of greater Catholic discipline and social understanding in matters of race than Protestant individualism was repeated.

Cornel West's policy recommendations do not move far from Niebuhr. West notes African Americans need more love and more money. Niebuhr would say they need respect and resources. In fact the first recommendation in the Detroit mayor's report pointed in the direction of building and restoring black housing. The need for housing policies was the subject of my first lecture at Union Theological Seminary in Roger Shinn's ethics class, and my first social activism in Pittsburgh was for the integration of the Construction Guilds. West's brilliant introduction to Niebuhr's classic of 1932, *Moral Man and Immoral Society,*[16] is on target. West's particular policies need the realism of William Julius Wilson who while less prophetic than West may be more relevant politically. His call for the renewal of the Works Progress Administration to overcome the poverty of the ghettos needs to be focused on housing.[17] Jimmy and Rosalyn Carter's Christian dedication in retirement to building housing is a profound clue to movement toward a solution. Many churches, including my own, are deeply involved in building and remodeling houses. Female leadership from our own minister and the director of East Liberty Development Corporation have been very successful in building new homes in Pittsburgh. Students from Pittsburgh Theological Seminary have had fulfilling vocations directing housing corporations. Niebuhr knew that housing was a central problem of racism. It was the

---

16. See West, "Foreword," in Niebuhr, *Moral Man,* xi–xiv.
17. Stone, *Political Crisis,* 166–67.

16. After King's Murder

fight over housing that shocked Detroit into learning that it had to deal with its racism. Our cities are getting old and housing built for the workers of the industrial revolution are worn out. In his disabled status from 1952 until his death in 1971, Ursula provided the home Reinhold depended upon, and helped edit some of his work. The new immigration movement needs housing. The United States has the resources that outshine the available money for the New Deal. Social forces are pushing in on the housing problems of the cities. The Build Back Better programs of President Biden and Vice President Harris had the correct title for America, but the Congress rejected the title and the programs. Reform takes patience as well as prudence, but in my perspective the time of *karios* is present for rebuilding America for the sake of employment and dignity. The launching of the campaign to provide every American with a home combines the passion of the social gospel and the realism of Niebuhr to provide the vision and politics of Martin Luther King Jr.

Bibliography

Baldwin, James. "The Fire Next Time." In *James Baldwin: Collected Essays*, edited by Toni Morrison, 291–348. New York: Library of America, 1998.
Bingham, June. *Courage to Change*. New York: Scribner, 1965.
Clark, Henry. *Serenity, Courage and Wisdom*. Cleveland: Pilgrim, 1994.
Cone, James H. *The Cross and the Lynching Tree*. Maryknoll, NY: Orbis, 2011.
———. *Said I Wasn't Gonna Tell Nobody: The Making of a Black Theologian*. Maryknoll, NY: Orbis, 2020.
Edwards, Herbert. "Niebuhr, Realism, and Civil Rights in America." *Christianity and Crisis* 46 (1986) 12–15.
———. "Racism and Christian Ethics in America." *Katallagete* (1971) 15–24.
Harland, Gordon. *The Thought of Reinhold Niebuhr*. New York: Oxford University Press, 1960.
Fox, W. Richard. *Reinhold Niebuhr: A Biography*. New York: Pantheon, 1985.
Griswold, Erwin N. *Law and Lawyers in the United States*. Cambridge: Harvard University Press, 1965.
Hannah-Jones, Nikole. "1619 Project." *New York Times Magazine*, August 18, 2019.
Horton, Miles. *The Long Haul: An Autobiography*. New York: Teacher's College Press, 1997.
King, Martin Luther King, Jr. "Eulogy for the Martyred Children." In *A Testament of Hope: The Essential Writings of Martin Luther King, Jr.*, edited by James Washington, 221–23. San Francisco: Harper & Row, 1986.
———. "Letter From a Birmingham Jail." *Christianity and Crisis* 23 (May 27, 1963) 89–91.
"Ku Klux Klan Assailed by Detroit Ministers." *Detroit Times*, November 2, 1925.
Minear, Paul. "My Peace." In *Reformed Faith and Politics*, edited by Ronald H. Stone, 31–48. Washington, DC: University Press of America, 1983.
Neuhaus, John Richard, ed. *Reinhold Niebuhr Today*. Grand Rapids: William B. Eerdmans, 1989.
Niebuhr, Reinhold. "An American Dilemma." *Christianity and Society* 9 (Summer 1944) 42.
———. "Bad Days at Little Rock." *Christianity and Crisis* 17 (October 14, 1957) 131.

BIBLIOGRAPHY

———. "Billy Graham Campaign." *Messenger* 22 (June 4, 1957) 5.
———. "Brief Comments." *Radical Religion* 3 (1937) 8–9.
———. *Children of Light and Children of Darkness.* New York: Scribner, 1944.
———. "Christian Faith and the Race Problem." *Christianity and Society* 10 (Spring 1945) 21–24.
———. "Christian Resources and Integration." *Lutheran* 38 (April 11, 1956) 23–24.
———. "Church and State South Africa." *Advance* 149 (September 6, 1957) 6.
———. "Church and the South African Tragedy." *Christianity and Crisis* 20 (May 2, 1960) 53–54.
———. "Church Council, To the." Reinhold Niebuhr Papers, Library of Congress, January 22, 1929.
———. "Civil Rights Bill." *New Leader* 40 (September 16, 1957) 9–11.
———. "Civil Rights Climax in Alabama." *Christianity and Crisis* 25 (April 5, 1965) 61.
———. "Civil Rights and Democracy." *Christianity and Crisis* 17 (July 8, 1957) 89.
———. "Civil Rights and the Filibuster." *Christianity and Crisis* 19 (February 2, 1959) 2–3.
———. "Complexity of the Race Issue." *Messenger* 21 (August 7, 1956) 5.
———. "Confessions of a Tired Radical." *Christian Century* 45 (August 30, 1928) 1046–47.
———. "Crisis in Protestantism." *Christian Century* 80 (December 4, 1963) 1499.
———. "Decision on Separation." *Lutheran* 36 (July 14, 1954) 13–14.
———. "Delta Cooperative Farm." *Radical Religion* 4 (Winter 1938) 7.
———. "Desegregation Issue." *Christianity and Society* 21 (Spring 1955) 3–4.
———. *Does Civilization Need Religion?* New York: Macmillan, 1927.
———. "Editorial Notes." *Christianity and Crisis* 4 (March 20, 1944) 2.
———. "Effect of the Supreme Court Decision." *Christianity and Crisis* 17 (February 4, 1957) 3.
———. "Ex Cathedra." *World Tomorrow* 16 (January 1933) 2.
———. "Fair Employment Practices Act." *Christianity and Crisis* 10 (Summer 1950) 3–5.
———. "The Fate of the Negro Minority in a Self-Righteous Nation." *Social Action* xxxv (1968) 43–64.
———. "Foreword." In *Dr. Martin Luther King Jr. et al. Speak on the War in Vietnam*, 3. New York: Clergy and Laity Concerned about Vietnam, 1967.
———. "Foreword." In *Mississippi Black Paper*, by Reinhold Niebuhr et al., n.p. New York: Random House, 1965.
———. "Fundraising Letter." Reinhold Niebuhr Papers, Library of Congress, May 27, 1932.
———. "Glimpses of the Southland." *Christian Century* 47 (July 16, 1930) 893–95.
———. "Heightened Racial Tensions." *Christianity and Crisis* 4 (March 20, 1944) 2.

BIBLIOGRAPHY

———."If Races 'Mix' Won't There Be Intermarriage?" *The Lutheran* (August 8, 1956) 17–18.

———. "Indicting Two Generations." *New Leader* 53 (October 5, 1970) 13–14.

———. "Intractability of Race Prejudice." *Christianity and Crisis* 22 (October 29, 1962) 181.

———. "Jews After the War." In *Love and Justice: Selections from the Shorter Writings of Reinhold Niebuhr*, edited by D. B. Robertson, 129–44. Philadelphia: Westminster, 1979.

———. "Justice to the American Negro." In *Pious and Secular America*, by Reinhold Niebuhr, 129–44. New York: Charles Scribner's Sons, 1958.

———. "The Kingdom of God and the Struggle for Social Justice." In *The Nature and Destiny of Man*, 244–86. New York: Charles Scribner's Sons, 1943.

———. "King's Chapel and the King's Court." *Christianity and Crisis* 29 (August 4, 1969) 211–12.

———. *Leaves from the Notebook of a Tamed Cynic*. New York: Willett and Clark, 1929.

———. "Liberty and Equality." In *Reformed Faith and Politics*, edited by Ronald H. Stone, 157–98. Washington, DC: University Press of America, 1983.

———. *Man's Nature and His Communities*. New York: Scribner, 1963.

———. "Man, the Unregenerate Tribalist." *Christianity and Crisis* 24 (July 6, 1964) 133–34.

———. "Meaning of the Tragedy in Birmingham." Reinhold Niebuhr Papers, Library of Congress, 1963.

———. "Meditations from Mississippi." *Christian Century* 54 (February 10, 1937) 183–84.

———. "Memorandum on Bicentennial." Reinhold Niebuhr Papers, Library of Congress, 1971.

———. "Mission and Opportunity: Religion in a Pluralistic Culture." In *Social Responsibility in an Age of Revolution*, edited by Louis Finkelstein, 177–211. New York: Jewish Theological Seminary, 1971.

———. "The Montgomery Savagery." *Christianity and Crisis* 21 (June 12, 1961) 103.

———. *Moral Man and Immoral Society: A Study in Ethics and Politics*. New York: Scribner, 1932.

———. "Moral Problems of Desegregation." *Evangelical Herald* 120 (November 27, 1955) 10.

———. "Mounting Racial Crisis." *Christianity and Crisis* 23 (July 8, 1963) 121–22.

———. "The Negro Dilemma." *New Leader* 43 (April 11, 1960) 13–14.

———. "Negroes and the Railroads." *Christianity and Society* 1 (Winter 1943) 11.

———. "The Negro in Detroit." Detroit Bureau of Governmental Research, Mayor's Interracial Committee, 1926. https://crcmich.org/wp-content/uploads/Negro_In_Detroit_OCR_OPT.pdf.

———. "Negro Issue in America." *Christianity and Society* 9 (Summer 1944) 5–7.
———. "Negro Minority and Its Fate in a Self-Righteous Nation." *Social Action* 35 (October 1968) 53–64.
———. "Notes on Myrdal's American Dilemma." *Christianity and Crisis* 4 (September 18, 1944) 2.
———. *Pious and Secular America*. New York: Charles Scribner's Sons, 1958.
———. "Proposal to Billy Graham." In *Love and Justice: Selections from the Shorter Writings of Reinhold Niebuhr*, edited by D. B. Robertson, 154–60. Philadelphia: Westminster, 1979.
———. "Question of Priorities." *New Leader* 53 (January 15, 1968) 9–11.
———. "Race and Christian Conscience." *Christianity and Crisis* 16 (July 23, 1956) 99.
———. "Race Issue." *Christianity and Society* 11 (Summer 1946) 6–7.
———. "Race Prejudice in the North." *Christian Century* xliv (May 12, 1947) 583–84.
———. "The Race Problem." *Christianity and Society* 3 (Summer 1942) 3–5.
———. *Reflections on the End of an Era*. New York: Scribner, 1934.
———. "Religion and the New Germany." *Christian Century* 50 (June 28, 1933) 845.
———. "The Religious Situation in America." In *Religion and Contemporary Society*, by Harold Stahmer, 145–55. New York: Macmillan, 1963.
———. "Review of Gunnar Myrdal: *An American Dilemma*." *Christianity and Crisis* 4 (September 18, 1944) 2.
———. "Rising Tide of Color." *New Leader* 44 (January 23, 1961) 16.
———. "School, Church and the Ordeals of Desegregation." *Christianity and Crisis* 16 (October 1, 1956) 121–22.
———. "School Issue in Editorial Notes." *Christianity and Crisis* 13 (February 2, 1953) 2.
———. "Segregation in the Schools and the Limits of the Law." *Christianity and Crisis* 12 (January 5, 1953) 178.
———. "Sin of Racial Prejudice." Religious News Service." *Messenger* 13 (February 1948) 6.
———. "South African Race Struggle." *Lutheran* 39 (August 21, 1957) 23.
———. "South African Racism." *Messenger* 17 (May 6, 1952) 7.
———. "South African Tragedy." *Christianity and Society* 2 (Spring 1955) 4–5.
———. "Southern Congressmen and the Anti-Lynching Bill." *Radical Religion* 3 (Winter 1937) 9.
———. "Sports and the Race Issue." *Messenger* 14 (February 1, 1949) 6.
———. *The Structure of Nations and Empires*. New York: Charles Scribner's Sons, 1959.
———. "The Supreme Court on Segregation in the Schools." *Christianity and Crisis* 14 (June 14, 1954) 75–77.
———. "Theologian's Comments on the Negro in America." *Reporter* 15 (November 29, 1956) 24–25.

BIBLIOGRAPHY

———. "This Is Prejudice." *Baltimore Sun* (October 11 and November 1, 1954) 13–15.

———. "Tragedy in South Africa." *Messenger* 22 (September 3, 1957) 5.

———. "Way of Non-violent Resistance." *Christianity and Society* 21 (Spring 1956) 3.

———. "What Resources Can the Christian Church Offer to Meet Crisis in Race Relations." *Messenger* 21 (April 3, 1956) 9.

———. "Why I Am Not a Christian." *Christian Century* 44 (1927) 1482.

"Pastors Urge Voters to Hit Klan Bigotry." *The Detroit Free Press* 91 (November 1, 1925) 1.

Paul, Pamela. "Antiracism Was Never the Right Answer." *New York Times*, October 6, 2023. https://www.nytimes.com/2023/10/05/opinion/ibram-x-kendi-racism.html.

"Report of the Mayor's Committee on Race Relations." Detroit, Michigan, 1926. https://archive.org/stream/reportofmayorscooounse/reportofmayorscooounse_djvu.txt.

Robertson, D. B., ed. *Love and Justice: Selections from the Shorter Writings of Reinhold Niebuhr*. Philadelphia: Westminster, 1979.

———. *Reinhold Niebuhr's Works*. Boston: G. K. Hall, 1979.

Stahmer, Harold, ed. *Religion and Contemporary Society*. New York: Macmillan, 1963.

Stone, Ronald. "Contribution of Reinhold Niebuhr to the Late Twentieth Century." In *Reinhold Niebuhr: His Religious, Social and Political Thought*, edited by Charles W. Kegley, 43–80. New York: Pilgrim, 1984.

———. "Niebuhr's Record on Race." *Christian Century* (February 2023) 7.

———. *The Political Crisis and Christian Ethics*. Eugene, OR: Wipf & Stock, 2023.

———. *Politics and Faith: Reinhold Niebuhr and Paul Tillich at Union Seminary in New York*. Macon: Mercer University Press, 2012.

———. *Reinhold Niebuhr in the 1960s*. Minneapolis: Fortress, 2019.

Surratt, Marshall. "Miles Horton." *Christianity and Crisis* (December 1990) 399.

Ward, Hiley. *Prophet of the Black Nation*. New York: Pilgrim, 1969.

West, Cornel. "Foreword." In *Moral Man and Immoral Society*, by Reinhold Niebuhr, xi–xiv. Louisville: Westminster John Knox, 2013.

———. *Race Maters*. Boston: Beacon, 1993.

West, Tracy C. "Racial Justice." In *The Oxford Handbook of Reinhold Niebuhr*, edited by Robin Lovin and Joshua Mauldin, 501–22. Oxford: Oxford University Press, 2021.

Wilkerson, Isabel. *Caste: The Origins of our Discontent*. New York: Random House, 2020.

Wilmore, Gayraud S. *Black and Presbyterian*. Philadelphia Geneva,1983.

Young, Andrew. "Speech at Testimonial Dinner for John C. Bennett." Reprinted in *Christianity and Crisis* 21 (May 3, 1971) 80.

Index

American Dilemma, The, 68, 78
Amos, 100
anti-lynching laws, 59
apartheid, 9, 71
Arab, 59

Baldwin, James, 13, 85–87
Bennett, John C., 73, 78
Bethel Evangelical Church, 12,
    13, 38, 39, 43, 57
    dispute, 40–41
Biden, Joseph, 107
bigotry, 65
Bingham, June, 66
Birmingham, 83
    bombing, 85–89
    whites of, 87
black authors, 104
black churches, 64, 86
black clashes, 21
black growth in Detroit, 21, 26
black minority, 97, 99
black nationalism, 38
Black Panthers, 104
black people, 21–40, 68, 72, 97
black population, 80
black power, 94
black revolution, 94, 97
blacks, 80, 94
Bonhoeffer, Dietrich, 50, 51
    Niebuhr's course, 95
boycott, 68

British Empire, 59
British racism, 73
brutality to Negroes, 25
Buber, Martin, 72
Butzel, Fred, 3, 19, 105

Calvinism, 76
caste, 93, 105
Chesnut, Robert, 1
Christ, 85, 86
Christian Century, The, 1, 43, 44
Christianity and Crisis, 81, 82
churches
civil rights, 63
    Act of 1957, 77–79
    proposed laws, 89
Christians, 2, 71–76, 86
Christian social ethics, 92
church, 86, 87, 95, 96
    black church, 83
    failures, 74, 81, 89
Cicero, 93
civil rights, 90, 93
    movement, 97
Civil War, 89, 94, 97
Cleage, Albert, 38
Clark, Henry, 74
Clergy and Laity Concerned
    About Vietnam, 95
colored people, 21–40
colored policemen, 26
communism, 59, 81

Index

Cone, James, 3, 10, 45, 51, 60–63, 74, 76, 81, 101
   seminar, 2
   Cross and the Lynching Tree, The, 2, 12
   Niebuhr's seminar, 95
   Said I Wasn't Gonna Tell Anyone, 5
"Confessions of a Tired Radical," 4, 37
Constitution, 93

Darrow, Clarence, 15
Declaration of Independence, 93
Delta Farm, 66, 80
Detroit, 21–38, 107
   newspapers, 3
Detroit Mayor's Commission on Race, 21, 94
   banks, 26–27
   black population, 19
   colored population growth, 21, 22, 26
   crime and police, 24–26
   church, 32, 33
   Bureau of Government Research, 21
   health, 29, 30
   housing, 21–23
   Negro community, 22
   Negro women, 31
   industry, 31
   Niebuhr's use in speeches, 36
   prejudice, 21
   recreation, 30–31
   welfare, 33
Does Civilization Need Religion?, 75

economic justice, 98
education, 93
Edwards, Herbert, 3, 73
Eddy, Sherwood, 45, 48, 51
ethics, 55, 110
equality, 66, 71, 75, 77

Fracker, Matthew, 2
Fascism, 57
Fellowship of Socialist Christians, 52, 57
Ford, Henry, 57
Ford Motor Company, 18
Fox, Richard, 3, 73
Franklin, Samuel, 51, 52

Gandhi, 37, 64
God, 82, 86
Graham, Billy, 74, 75

Harland, Gordon, 66
Harlem, 9, 82, 95
Harris, Kamala, 107
Horton, Miles, 47–49
   Highlander School, 48, 78, 80
   Highlander Center, 49
housing, 100
Humphrey, Herbert H., 66

idealism, 64, 75
integration, 75, 77
   of churches, 99
Institute of Advanced Study, 78, 90
Irony of American History, The, 1
international relations, 73, 74
Israel, 72

Jewish state, 59
Jewish Theological Seminary, 71, 91
Jews, 71–76
justice, 61, 65, 69, 71, 81, 86
   to blacks, 44
   injustice, 61
   in Mississippi, 89
   unattained by Negroes, 24

Index

Jesus, 50, 55
Johnson, Lyndon, 5, 77, 84, 96
Judaism, 59, 71, 76

King, Martin Luther, Jr., 8, 12, 38, 45, 60, 63, 64, 77
  church, 81
  illusions, 75
  "Letter from a Birmingham Jail," 83
  March on Washington, 100
  Niebuhr's praise, 87
  realism, 75
  vision, 107
Kingdom of God, 55, 61
"King's Chapel and King's Court," 100
Ku Klux Klan, 3, 15, 16, 52, 77
Keppel-Compton, Urusla, 50
Kerner Commission, 3, 39
Kilgore, James, 85

liberalism, 55, 64
Liberal Party, 80
liberty, 7
Lord of love, 42
love, 42, 59, 68
Lincoln, Abraham, 15

Man's Nature and His Communities, 92
Marxism, 55
Marx, Karl, 97
Mayor's Inter-racial Committee, 3, 17–40, 106
Messianism, 72
Methodist Church, 8, 10
Mandela, Nelson, 80
Moral Man and Immoral Society, 42–47, 64, 83
Morgenthau, Hans, 90, 91
Mississippi Black Paper, 3, 89–91
Myrdahl, Gunnar, 84

National Advisory Commission, 98, 99
Nature and Destiny of Man, The, 7, 60, 90, 106
Nazism, 57, 77, 81
Negative Income Tax, 99
Negro, 65, 100
"Negro Minority and It's Fate in a Self-Righteous Nation, The," 98
Niebuhr, H. Richard, 38
Niebuhr, Reinhold
  aging, 86
  antisemitism, 57
  black people, 44
  boycotts, 54
  Christian Gospel, 39
  church failures, 53
  Delta Cooperative Farm, 51, 52
  defense of Martin Luther King Jr., 95, 96
  Detroit, 43, 54
  education, 55
  ethics, 50
  Gandhi, 44
  housing, 55
  idealism, 43, 64
  international relations, 10, 54
  "Jews and Christians," 71–76
  liberalism, 55
  lynching, 3, 41, 52, 57, 10
  Marxist criticism, 43
  Negro race, 44
  nonviolent resistance, 44
  politics, 60
  power, 50
  poverty, 97
  racial justice, 97
  realism, 67
  Supreme Court, 69, 75, 94
  tribalism, 92
Niebuhr, Urusla, 59, 66, 78, 90, 105

Index

Nixon, Richard, 101
   Niebuhr's critique, 100
nuclear war, 81, 83
nonviolent campaign, 64, 83

Palestine, 59–62
Parks, Rosa, 48, 49
Peale, Norman Vincent, 74
Pittsburgh Theological
   Seminary, 2 10, 11
plutocrats, 75
Pious and Secular America, 71, 79
politics, 94
   of King, 107
power, 61, 75
prejudice, 88
pride, 65
proletariat, 94
prophets, 72
Protestant Churches, 69
public schools, 66, 68, 69
Providence Farm, 52

race, 65
racial arrogance, 68, 71
racial justice, 88, 97
racism, 1, 17–40, 65
Radical Religion, 57, 60
realism, 64, 75
religion, 92
Robertson, D. B, 65
Roberts, Samuel, 10
Roman Catholic, 69, 95
Roosevelt, Franklin D., 57
Russia, 59, 82

segregation, 88
Shinn, Roger, 81, 90, 196
sin, 65, 68
slavery, 1, 55, 104
Smith, James A., 1
social action, 50
social gospel, 38, 62–64, 106

social justice, 74
Soviet Union, 1, 73
Stone, Randall, 5
Stone Ronald H., 66
   Allegheny County
      Commission, 10
   Dakota City, Iowa, 5
   heritage, 5
   Humboldt County, 4, 5
   Riverside Church, 9
   Sioux City, 6
   teaching, 2
   Allegheny County
      Commission, 10
   Riverside Church, 9
Students for a Democratic
   Society, 102
Supreme Court, 67–69, 79, 94

Thomas, Norman, 5
Tillich, Paul, 78
toleration, 71
tribalism, 91–93
Troeltsch, Ernst, 18
Truman, Harry S., 5, 59, 66

unionization, 75
Union Theological Seminary, 2, 7, 10, 51, 105

Vietnam War, 45, 60, 95–98, 102
violence, 44
voting, 69, 77, 98

war, 43
West, Cornel, 106
West, Tracy, 105
wartime essays, 41
White Citizens Council, 52
white resistance, 94
white sin, 3
white writers, 94
World Council of Churches, 82

Index

World Tomorrow, The, 40, 43, 50, 51, 54

Zionist, 59

www.ingramcontent.com/pod-product-compliance
Lightning Source LLC
Chambersburg PA
CBHW031347160426
43196CB00007B/759